THE HISTORY OF
EASTERN EUROPE
FOR BEGINNERS™

WRITERS AND READERS PUBLISHING, INC.

P.O. Box 461, Village Station
New York, NY 10014

Writers and Readers Limited
9 Cynthia Street
London N1 9JF
England

•

Text and Illustrations Copyright: © 1997 Paul Beck, Edward Mast and Perry Tapper
Book Design: Paul Beck, Edward Mast and Perry Tapper
Cover Illustration: Paul Beck
Cover Design: Terrie Dunkelberger

A Writers and Readers Documentary Comic Book
Copyright © 1997
ISBN # 0-86316-237-1 Trade
1 2 3 4 5 6 7 8 9 0

Manufactured in the United States of America

Beginners Documentary Comic Books are published by Writers and Readers Publishing, Inc. Its trademark, consisting of the words "For Beginners, Writers and Readers Documentary Comic Books" and the Writers and Readers logo, is registered in the U. S. Patent and Trademark Office and in other countries.

Writers and Readers—
publishing FOR BEGINNERS™ books
continuously since 1975:

1975: Cuba • 1976: Marx • 1977: Lenin • 1978: Nuclear Power • 1979: Einstein • Freud • 1980: Mao • Trotsky • 1981: Capitalism • 1982: Darwin • Economists • French Revolution • Marx's Kapital • French Revolution • Food • Ecology • 1983: DNA • Ireland • 1984: London • Peace • Medicine • Orwell • Reagan • Nicaragua • Black History • 1985: Marx Diary • 1986: Zen • Psychiatry • Reich • Socialism • Computers • Brecht • Elvis • 1988: Architecture • Sex • JFK • Virginia Woolf • 1990: Nietzsche • Plato • Malcolm X • Judaism • 1991: WW II • Erotica • African History • 1992:Philosophy • Rainforests • Malcolm X • Miles Davis • Islam • Pan Africanism • 1993: Psychiatry • Black Women • Arabs & Israel • Freud • 1994: Babies • Foucault • Heidegger • Hemingway • Classical Music • 1995: Jazz • Jewish Holocaust • Health Care • Domestic Violence • Sartre • United Nations • Black Holocaust • Black Panthers • Martial Arts • History of Clowns • 1996: Opera • Biology • Saussure • UNICEF • Kierkegaard • Addiction & Recovery • I Ching • Buddha • Derrida • Chomsky • McLuhan • Jung • 1997: Lacan • Shakespeare • Structuralism

---

THE HISTORY OF
EASTERN EUROPE
FOR BEGINNERS™

PAUL BECK, EDWARD MAST,
PERRY TAPPER

Writers and Readers

TABLE OF CONTENTS

Paul Beck is a cartoonist and graphic artist, creator of the annual MOOSE-A-MONTH calendar. Paul is of Hungarian descent, and he has degrees in Linguistics, music, and psychology.

Ed Mast is a writer and playwright. His plays have been performed in New York, Chicago, Washington DC, Seattle, Tashkent, London, and other cities. His publications include THE LOVE SONGS OF MISTER ATOM, a series of poems inspired by the life of J. Robert Oppenheimer.

Perry Tapper has studied History at Northeastern University, Boston, and Palacky University in the Czech Republic, where he currently lives with his wife and three children. Perry is the author of WHO ARE WE: TALES OF NATIONAL IDENTITY and the upcoming PRACTICING THE PAST: A SHORT HISTORY OF THE UNITED STATES, as well as a translation of J. Pekar's HISTORY OF CZECHOSLOVAKIA.

PROLOGUE

SINCE THE COLLAPSE OF THE COMMUNIST SYSTEM IN EUROPE AND THE SOVIET UNION IN 1988-89, EASTERN EUROPE HAS BEEN RUMBLING WITH ACTIVITY...

RUMBLE!

CLATTER

AN EXPERT

THERE WAS TURMOIL BE-FORE THEN OF COURSE, BUT JUST SINCE 1988...

...EASTERN EUROPE HAS BEEN IN THE NEWS NEARLY EVERY DAY.

MOST OF US KNOW VERY LITTLE ABOUT THESE COUNTRIES.

POP QUIZ!

1. WHAT COUNTRIES BORDER BULGARIA?
2. WHAT IS THE CAPITAL OF ALBANIA?
3. WHAT IS THE OFFICIAL LANGUAGE OF SLOVAKIA?
4. LIST 3 PRINCIPAL EXPORTS OF HUNGARY
5. WHAT COUNTRIES WERE FORMERLY PART OF YUGOSLAVIA?
6. WHAT IS THE NAME OF THE POLISH CURRENCY?
7. WHAT IS THE RULING PARTY IN THE CZECH REPUBLIC?
8. WHERE CAN YOU BUY PARTS FOR YOUR YUGO?

WITH SO MANY DIFFERENT, OVERLAPPING ISSUES AT STAKE IN THE REGION, IT'S HARD TO KEEP TRACK OF **WHO'S** IN CONFLICT WITH **WHOM** OVER **WHAT.**

SO... TO UNDERSTAND THE SOURCES OF CONFLICT IN EASTERN EUROPE,

WHERE SHOULD WE BEGIN?

SHOULD WE START WITH...

AH! THE BEGINNINGS ARE SHROUDED IN A VEIL OF MYSTERY!

...OR IS THAT "VEILED IN A SHROUD OF MYSTERY"...?

THE FALL OF COMMUNISM?

IS THAT REALLY WHEN IT ALL STARTED, OR IS IT JUST WHEN PROBLEMS CAME TO THE SURFACE?

OR HOW ABOUT...

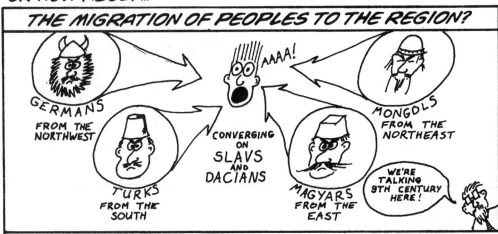

THE MIGRATION OF PEOPLES TO THE REGION?

GERMANS FROM THE NORTHWEST

AAAA!

MONGOLS FROM THE NORTHEAST

TURKS FROM THE SOUTH

CONVERGING ON SLAVS AND DACIANS

MAGYARS FROM THE EAST

WE'RE TALKING 9TH CENTURY HERE!

HAS THERE REALLY BEEN TROUBLE EVER SINCE THEN?

HOW ABOUT STARTING WHEN THE MOLTEN SURFACE OF THE EARTH BEGAN TO COOL?

WHO ARE WE, JAMES MICHENER?

HOW ABOUT...

4

...THE END OF WORLD WAR ONE

WORLD WAR ONE? WHY NOT WORLD WAR TWO? OR THE FRANCO-PRUSSIAN WAR? WHY A WAR AT ALL?

WORLD WAR ONE? HAD THE LAVA COOLED YET?

WHY THE END OF WORLD WAR ONE? BECAUSE, WITH THE TREATIES OF VERSAILLES, NEUILLY, AND ST. GERMAIN, LAND WAS REDISTRIBUTED, NATIONS WERE CREATED, AND THE VICTORIOUS ALLIES DREW UP...

THE MODERN MAP OF EUROPE

...WHICH LASTED FOR MOST OF THE 20TH CENTURY

REALLY? WHERE DID ALL OF THIS HAPPEN, AND WHEN?

CHAPTER ONE

PARIS, 1919

THE END OF THE WAR TO END ALL WARS

IN 1918, AT THE END OF FOUR YEARS OF WAR, EUROPE WAS A SHAMBLES. EMPIRES HAD BEEN BROKEN APART...

R.I.P. OTTOMAN EMPIRE

R.I.P. GERMANY (WAR LOSER)

R.I.P. AUSTRO-HUNGARIAN EMPIRE (WAR LOSER)

R.I.P. RUSSIAN EMPIRE (INTERNAL CAUSES)

THE VICTORS GATHERED IN PARIS TO DETERMINE THE OUTCOME OF THE WAR TO END ALL WARS. NOT TO MENTION DIVIDING UP THE HUGE AREAS OF LAND THAT WERE UP FOR GRABS.

THERE WERE SEVERAL TREATIES, THE MOST PROFOUND AND FAR-REACHING OF WHICH WAS SIGNED AT THE PALACE OF *VERSAILLES.*

REPRESENTATIVES OF 32 NATIONS GATHERED HERE. AMONG THE NATIONS WERE MANY NEW COUNTRIES, INVENTED FROM THE RUBBLE OF FORMER EMPIRES. (THE LOSERS WEREN'T INVITED, NOR WAS COMMUNIST RUSSIA.)

SO THESE 32 DELEGATES DREW UP THE MODERN MAP OF EUROPE?

NOT PRECISELY...

7

THE POWER TO DIVIDE UP EASTERN EUROPE - THE REAL *DECISION-MAKING* POWER - LAY WITH FOUR PEOPLE. THE "BIG FOUR" REPRESENTED THE WAR'S WINNERS.

VITTORIO ORLANDO
ITALIAN PREMIER

GEORGES CLEMENCEAU
FRENCH PREMIER

DAVID LLOYD GEORGE
BRITISH PRIME MINISTER

WOODROW WILSON
UNITED STATES PRESIDENT

SO THESE FOUR WORLD LEADERS USED THEIR VAST, DETAILED KNOWLEDGE OF THE POLITICAL, SOCIAL, AND GEOGRAPHIC MAKEUP OF THE AREA TO DRAW UP THE MAP, RIGHT?

NOT PRECISELY...

WHERE'S TRANSYLVANIA?

HMM...WHO WANTS IT?

I THINK IT'S OVER HERE...

THE ROMANIANS, I THINK...

WE'RE NOT MAKING THIS UP! THE BIG FOUR ACTUALLY SPREAD A MAP OUT ON THE FLOOR AND GOT DOWN ON THEIR HANDS AND KNEES TO TRY TO DETERMINE WHERE THE NEW BORDERS WOULD GO.

THEY WEREN'T FAMILIAR WITH THE AREA?

CERTAINLY NOT AS FAMILIAR AS THE FORMER IMPERIAL POWERS OF GERMANY, AUSTRIA-HUNGARY, AND RUSSIA. BUT *THEY* WEREN'T INVITED TO THE CONFERENCE.

WHAT ABOUT THE PEOPLE WHO LIVED THERE?

11

THERE WERE 28 DELEGATES DECIDING THE FATE OF EASTERN EUROPE - *BUT:*

ONLY FIVE WERE *FROM* EASTERN EUROPE. EVERYONE ELSE WAS LEFT IN THE BACKGROUND.

SO...

CHAPTER TWO

MEET THE SLAVS

WHO ARE THE SLAVS?

BUT THE PEOPLE WHO SPREAD THE FARTHEST AND STAYED THE LONGEST CAME FROM THE PROVINCE OF GALICIA, AN AREA IN WHAT IS NOW EASTERN POLAND AND WESTERN UKRAINE. THESE PEOPLE HAD LIVED IN THE AREA OF GALICIA FOR NEARLY 20,000 YEARS.

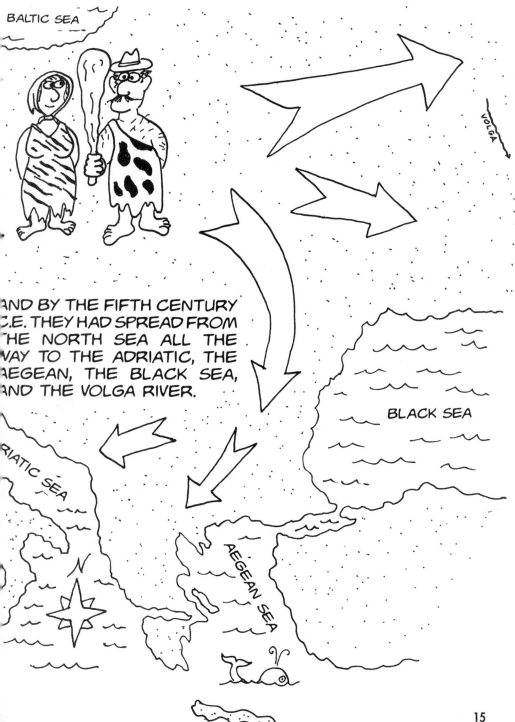

BALTIC SEA

VOLGA

AND BY THE FIFTH CENTURY C.E. THEY HAD SPREAD FROM THE NORTH SEA ALL THE WAY TO THE ADRIATIC, THE AEGEAN, THE BLACK SEA, AND THE VOLGA RIVER.

BLACK SEA

ADRIATIC SEA

AEGEAN SEA

THE SLAVS' BEGINNINGS ARE LOST IN THE CLOUDY MISTS OF PREHISTORY! OR IS THAT "THE MISTY CLOUDS..."?

WE DON'T KNOW ALL THAT MUCH ABOUT THESE EARLY PEOPLES, THOUGH WE DO KNOW THAT THEY WERE *PAGANS*.

"PAGAN" IS A NASTY ROMAN WORD WHICH ORIGINALLY MEANT "VILLAGER" BUT CAME TO MEAN "IGNORANT PEASANT WHO WORSHIPS DOPEY GODS".

AMONG THE LOCAL DEITIES WERE *SVAROG*, THE FATHER OF THE GODS, AND A GREAT DUALISTIC PAIR: *BYELOBOG*, THE WHITE GOD, AND *CHERNOBOG*, THE BLACK GOD.

IN THE NINTH CENTURY C.E., THE GREEK CHRISTIAN MISSIONARIES, CYRIL AND METHODIUS, WERE SENT TO THE EASTERN ROMAN EMPIRE...

...TO CONVERT SOME OF THESE "IGNORANT PEASANTS WHO WORSHIP DOPEY GODS."

TO HELP CONVERT THE NATIVES, CYRIL AND METHODIUS NEEDED TO TRANSLATE CHRISTIAN LITERATURE INTO THE LOCAL LANGUAGES. AT THE TIME, THESE LOCAL LANGUAGES HAD NO CONSISTENT WRITTEN FORM, SO CYRIL AND METHODIUS DEVELOPED A NEW ALPHABET, WHICH BECAME KNOWN AS...

17

THE *CYRILLIC* ALPHABET (DERIVED FROM GREEK).

АБВГДЕЕЁЖЗИЙ
КЛМНОПРСТУФ
ХЦЧШЩЪЫЬЭЮЯ

WITH THIS ALPHABET, THEY GAVE WRITTEN FORM TO AN OLD VERSION OF THE RUSSIAN LANGUAGE, WHICH THEY CALLED *SLAVONIC*, AFTER THE PEOPLE OF THE AREA, WHO BY THE NINTH CENTURY HAD COME TO BE CALLED *SLAVS*.

(UGLY ETYMOLOGY NOTE:
OUR WORD "SLAVE" DERIVES FROM THE WORD "SLAV", BECAUSE SO MANY SLAVS WERE ENSLAVED DURING THE MIDDLE AGES BY THE HOLY ROMAN EMPIRE.)

SO ALL THE SLAVS USE THE CYRILLIC ALPHABET?

NO! SOME OF US USE THE ROMAN ALPHABET.

WHY?

CYRIL AND METHODIUS WERE CHRISTIAN MISSIONARIES, BUT IN THAT TIME THERE WERE TWO DIFFERENT FACTIONS STRUGGLING FOR DOMINANCE WITHIN THE CHRISTIAN CHURCH. CYRIL AND METHODIUS BELONGED TO THE *EASTERN* FACTION, WHICH HAD ITS ROOTS IN BYZANTIUM—OR THE EASTERN ROMAN EMPIRE—AND WAS LED BY FOUR PATRIARCHS. THE WESTERN FACTION WAS FOUNDED IN ROME...

ME NOW?

WILL YOU BE *QUIET*?

...AND WAS LED BY A POPE.

PATRIARCH

POPE

THE TWO FACTIONS DISAGREED ON MANY FUNDAMENTAL AND IMPORTANT PRINCIPLES, SUCH AS...

...HOW MANY FINGERS TO HOLD UP FOR A BLESSING

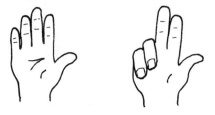

...WHETHER TO GIVE COMMUNION BY HAND OR WITH A SPOON

...WHAT HAT TO WEAR

...WHICH CALENDAR TO USE, WHICH LANGUAGE TO USE, AND

WHO WAS BOSS!

N 1054, THE EASTERN AND WESTERN FACTIONS OF THE CHURCH SPLIT ALTOGETHER INTO THE **EASTERN OR- THODOX CHURCH** AND THE **ROMAN CATHOLIC CHURCH**. MEANWHILE, BOTH CHURCHES HAD MANY CONVERTS AMONG THE SLAVS

(AND MEANWHILE, CHERNOBOG AND BYELOBOG WERE HISTORY.)

CYRIL AND METHODIUS WERE FROM THE EASTERN CHURCH, SO THE EASTERN ORTHODOX CONVERTS USED THE CYRILLIC ALPHABET.

THE ROMAN CATHOLIC CONVERTS, HOWEVER, LEARNED THE ROMAN ALPHABET (THE ONE YOU'RE READING).

SO...

AS A RESULT OF THESE AND OTHER INFLUENCES, TH
SLAVS SPREAD OUT IN THREE DISTINCT BUT OVERLAPPIN
BRANCHES...

THE EAST SLAVS:

RUSSIANS
UKRAINIANS
BYELORUSSIANS

THE EAST SLAVS HAVE ALWAYS BEEN CULTUR- ALLY AND POLITICALLY ORIENTED TOWARD ASIA. THEY ARE PRIMARILY RUSSIAN ORTHODOX AND USE THE CYRILLIC AL- PHABET

ORIENTED TOWARD ASIA! HAW HAW!

THE WEST SLAVS:

- POLES
- CZECHS
- SLOVAKS
- LETTS
- LITHUANIANS
- MOLDAVIANS
- RUTHENIANS

THE WEST SLAVS HAVE AL-
WAYS SEEN THEMSELVES
AS ALLIED TO THE WEST-
ERN EUROPEAN POWERS.

SO WOULD THAT MAKE
THEM *OCCIDENTED* TO-
WARD THE WEST?

SOME OF THEM, SUCH AS THE MOLDAVIANS AND
SOME SLOVAKS, WERE TRADITIONALLY ORTHODOX;
BUT THE MAJORITY HAVE ALWAYS BEEN ROMAN
CATHOLICS OR, IN THE CASE OF THE LETTS AND A
NUMBER OF CZECHS, PROTESTANT.
VIRTUALLY ALL USE THE ROMAN ALPHABET.

THE SOUTH SLAVS:

SERBS
CROATS
SLOVENES
BOSNIANS
BULGARIANS*

*THE BULGARIANS ARE ACTUALLY DESCENDED BOTH FROM SOUTH SLAVS AND *BULGARS*, A NON-SLAVIC PEOPLE WHO INVADED THE AREA IN THE NINTH CENTURY, C.E.

THE SOUTH SLAVS ARE A PRETTY SPLINTERY BRANCH:

BULGARIANS AND SERBS USE THE CYRILLIC ALPHABET.

CROATS AND SLOVENES USE THE ROMAN ALPHABET.

BOSNIANS USE *BOTH* ALPHA-BETS.

MANY BOSNIANS ARE *MUSLIMS*, HAVING CONVERTED TO ISLAM IN THE 14TH CENTURY.

SO IS EVERYONE IN EASTERN EUROPE A SLAV?

NO!

SOME, LIKE THE MONGOLS, HUNS, TATARS AND AVARS WERE INVADERS WHO DIDN'T STAY LONG.

SOME CAME FROM OTHER PLACES AND STAYED. FOR EXAMPLE, THE **MAGYARS** CAME FROM 1000 MILES EAST, BRINGING WITH THEM THE NON-SLAVIC LANGUAGE AND CULTURE THAT BECAME **MODERN HUNGARIAN**.

THE HUNGARIAN LANGUAGE BELONGS TO THE **FINNO-UGRIAN** LANGUAGE FAMILY. THE SLAVIC LANGUAGES BELONG TO THE **INDO-EUROPEAN** LANGUAGE FAMILY. SO DOES ENGLISH.

SOME NON-SLAVIC PEOPLE WERE THERE BEFORE THE SLAVS ARRIVED-
THE ROMANIANS, ORIGINALLY CALLED THE VLACHS, WERE ALREADY IN THE REGION OF MODERN ROMANIA AS FAR BACK AS 1900 B.C.E. (BEFORE COMMON ERA). THE ROMANIAN LANGUAGE IS DESCENDED FROM THE LATIN OF THE ROMANS, FROM THE TIME WHEN THE AREA WAS PART OF THE ROMAN EMPIRE.

NOW?

NOT YET!

THE ALBANIANS ARE ALSO AN ANCIENT PEOPLE, DATING BACK AT LEAST TO THE ROMAN PROVINCE CALLED ILLYRICUM. THEIR LANGUAGE IS NOT SLAVIC, ALTHOUGH IT IS IN THE INDO-EUROPEAN LANGUAGE FAMILY.

BECAUSE OF ITS GEOGRAPHICAL POSITION AT THE CROSSROADS OF EUROPE, SCANDINAVIA, ASIA, AND THE MIDDLE EAST, THIS REGION OF THE WORLD HAS ALWAYS BEEN A MEETING PLACE, INTERSECTION, MELTING POT, AND FLASHPOINT FOR ALL SORTS OF...

PEOPLE

ARMIES

MIGRATIONS

ATTACKS

RETREATS

NEGOTIATIONS

EMPIRES

REVOLUTIONS...

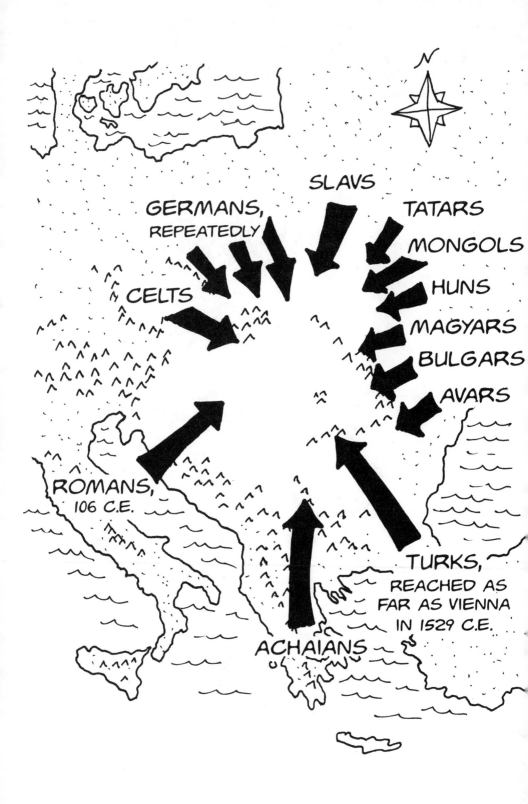

THIS.

GERMANS

GERMANS
POLES

SLOVAKS
CZECHS POLES
SLOVAKS
UKRAINIANS
HUNGARIANS SLOVAKS
HUNGARIANS
GERMANS
HUNGARIANS GERMANS
HUNGARIANS
SLOVENES ROMANIANS
CROATS CROATS GERMANS
SERBS BOSNIAKS
SERBS SERBS
BOSNIAKS
CROATS TURKS
BOSNIAKS ALBAN-
MONTENEGRINS IANS BULGARIANS
ALBANIANS MACE- TURKS
DONIANS
TURKS MACEDONIANS
GREEKS

WHY?
BECAUSE THE REGION HAS ALSO HAD TO CONTEND
WITH...

NOW? NOW

30

CHAPTER THREE

EMPIRES

OVER THE CENTURIES, VARIOUS PARTS OF EASTERN EUROPE HAVE RULED BY EMPIRES:

THE ROMAN EMPIRE

THE EMPEROR TRAJAN INVADED IN 106 C.E.

ROMANS LEFT THE AREA IN 274 C.E.

THE WESTERN ROMAN EMPIRE FELL IN 456 C.E.

THE BYZANTINE (OR EASTERN ROMAN) EMPIRE

THE EASTERN EMPIRE, WITH ITS CAPITAL IN CONSTANTINOPLE, SPLIT OFF FROM THE WESTERN EMPIRE IN 395 C.E. IT HAD ITS UPS AND DOWNS FOR OVER 1000 YEARS AND FINALLY FELL IN 1453 TO...

THE OTTOMAN EMPIRE,
CENTERED IN TURKEY

THE TURKS SWEPT THROUGH THE BALKANS IN 1090, WON MOST OF SOUTHEASTERN EUROPE AT THE BATTLE OF KOSOVO IN 1398, INHERITED THE DOMAINS FROM BYZANTIUM IN 1453, LOST SOME TO THE RUSSIANS IN THE 1800'S, AND WERE A MUSLIM PRESENCE IN THE REGION UNTIL WORLD WAR ONE.

NOT TO MENTION...

THE HOLY ROMAN EMPIRE

WHICH WAS ACTUALLY A SE-
RIES OF NOT-VERY-WELL-
ORGANIZED ATTEMPTS TO
REINVENT THE ROMAN EM-
PIRE, STARTING IN FRANCE
AND GERMANY. CHARLE-
MAGNE BEGAN TRYING IN
THE 800'S, AND PEOPLE
KEPT TRYING FOR 1000
YEARS, THOUGH IN FACT
THIS EMPIRE MORE OR
LESS DEGENERATED INTO...

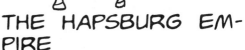

THE HAPSBURG EM-PIRE

THE HAPSBURG FAMILY
RULED AUSTRIA FROM 1282
TO 1918. THEY INTERMAR-
RIED WITH RULING FAMI-
LIES FROM RUSSIA TO
ENGLAND TO SPAIN, HOLD-
ING ONTO THE LANDS LIKE
A FAMILY ESTATE AND IN-
VENTING THE PHRASE
"WHERE THE SUN NEVER
SETS" TO DESCRIBE THEIR
LANDS. A FEW OF THEM
WERE HOLY ROMAN EM-
PERORS. NEGOTIATIONS
WITH SOME VERY PUSHY
MAGYARS TURNED THIS
EMPIRE INTO...

THE AUSTRO-HUN-GARIAN EMPIRE

WHICH BEGAN IN 1867,
KEPT UP THE CENTURIES-
OLD BATTLE AGAINST THE
OTTOMAN TURKS, SIDED
WITH GERMANY IN WORLD
WAR I, AND CONSE-
QUENTLY FELL IN 1918.

"...THE GREAT AUSTRIAN
EMPIRE, CAESARIAN HEIR
TO OVERLORDING ROME..."
-HERMAN MELVILLE, MOBY DICK

AND THAT
AIN'T ALL!

THE FRENCH (NAPOLEONIC) EMPIRE

NAPOLEON SEVERELY WEAKENED THE HAPSBURG EMPIRE BY CONQUERING MOST OF EUROPE. HE THEN CROWNED HIMSELF EMPEROR IN 1804. NAPOLEON MARCHED THROUGH POLAND TO ATTACK RUSSIA. (A BAD IDEA, AS IT TURNED OUT; BUT THAT'S ANOTHER STORY.)

THE PRUSSIAN EMPIRE

WHICH TOOK SHAPE IN THE LATE 1600'S, MAKING INROADS INTO POLAND, AUSTRIA, AND THE CZECH LANDS. IN 1871 PRUSSIA BECAME THE UNIFIED STATE OF GERMANY, WHOSE EMPIRE LASTED UNTIL 1918. HOWEVER, THIS IS NOT TO BE CONFUSED WITH...

THE GERMAN (NAZI) EMPIRE

WHICH ONLY LASTED FROM 1933 TO 1945 BUT MADE A *BIG* FUSS, CONQUERING POLAND, ANNEXING CZECHOSLOVAKIA, AUSTRIA, AND PARTS OF YUGOSLAVIA.

SHEESH! IS THERE NO END OF EMPIRES?

THE RUSSIAN EMPIRE

BEGAN AS THE KIEVAN STATE IN THE NINTH CENTURY AND EXPANDED MAINLY EASTWARD. THE RUSSIAN EMPIRE BATTLED AGAINST THE OTTOMANS, NAPOLEON, AUSTRIA-HUNGARY AND BRITAIN, AND FINALLY FELL AFTER 1000 YEARS TO THE BOLSHEVIKS IN 1917.

AFTER WORLD WAR TWO, THE RUSSIAN EMPIRE REAPPEARED AS...

THE SOVIET EMPIRE

WHICH LASTED UNTIL 1991-BUT MORE ABOUT THAT LATER.

DID ALL THESE EMPIRES MAKE THINGS BETTER, OR WORSE?

THAT DEPENDS ON WHOM YOU ASK...

ARE EMPIRES GOOD OR BAD?

WELL, THERE ARE ADVANTAGES AND DISADVANTAGES...

ADVANTAGES OF EMPIRE:

AQUEDUCTS

ROADS

TRAINS RUN ON TIME

A FEW PEOPLE LIVE HIGH ON THE HOG

PROTECTION FROM HUNS
" " MONGOLS
" " VISIGOTHS
" " TURKS
" " CRUSADERS

LAW 'N' ORDER

STANDARDIZATION OF LANGUAGE

STANDARDIZATION OF CULTURE

STANDARDIZATION OF RELIGION

DRAWBACKS OF EMPIRE:

TAXES

ABSENTEE RULERS

LOCAL RULE BY WHATEVER STOOGES ARE WILLING TO COLLABORATE

DICTATORSHIP

SUPPRESSION OF LOCAL CULTURE

SUPPRESSION OF LOCAL SELF-DETERMINATION

MILITARY CONSCRIPTION

STANDARDIZATION OF LANGUAGE

STANDARDIZATION OF CULTURE

STANDARDIZATION OF RELIGION

YOU MAKE THE CALL.

HERE'S HOW EMPIRES WORK:

EMPIRES RISE...

AND THEN, THEY *FALL*

WHEN EMPIRES RISE,
("RISE" IN THIS CASE MEANS "EXPAND")
THEY MAKE THEIR PRESENCE FELT IN *BIG* WAYS...

AND *LITTLE* WAYS

WITH EMPIRES COME:

NEW LAWS

HEAR YE THE NEW RULES:

RULE 1: THE EMPIRE IS THE BOSS

RULE 2: EVERY DAY WE WILL SAY, "THE EMPIRE IS THE BOSS"

RULE 3: REPEAT RULES 1 AND 2

NEW BUREAUCRACY
(WHICH IS SOMETIMES THE *OLD* BUREAUCRACY WITH A NEW SALARY)

I USED TO BE THE MAYOR, BUT NOW I'M THE *PROCURATOR*!

NEW TAXES

AQUEDUCTS DON'T GET BUILT FOR *FREE*, YOU KNOW!

AND SOMETIMES, *NEW RELIGION*.

TO EASTERN EUROPE,

THE ROMAN EMPIRE
BROUGHT *CATHOLICISM*,

THE BYZANTINE EMPIRE
BROUGHT EASTERN *OR-THODOX CHRISTIANITY*,

THE OTTOMAN EMPIRE
BROUGHT *ISLAM*,

AND THE PRUSSIAN EMPIRE
BROUGHT *PROTESTANTISM*.

SOMETIMES OTHER RELIGIONS WERE TOLERATED.
SOMETIMES NOT.

LOCAL CUSTOMS, LANGUAGE, CULTURE, AND SELF-DE-
TERMINATION IN GENERAL ARE USUALLY...

...DISCOURAGED, IF NOT OPENLY SUPPRESSED.

AND A KEY ELEMENT WITHIN EMPIRES:
PEOPLE ARE ENCOURAGED TO MOVE AROUND AND MIX TOGETHER

INSIDE AN EMPIRE, INTERNAL BOUNDARIES ARE RE-LAXED...

WITH BOUNDARIES RELAXED, PEOPLE MOVE FROM PLACE TO PLACE BECAUSE OF BAD ECONOMY, BAD POLITICS, BAD SOCIAL CONDITIONS, EVEN BAD WEATHER.

SOMETIMES PEOPLE ARE RELOCATED FOR MILITARY PURPOSES-

OF COURSE THIS CAUSES SOME SOCIAL PROBLEMS AMONG CITIZENS...

BUT JUST AS OFTEN, CITIZENS OF DIFFERENT REGIONS ARE UNITED BY A COMMON ENEMY:

44

BUT THEN, JUST WHEN SUBJECTS OF THE EMPIRE HAVE BEEN EDUCATED AND ARE BEGINNING TO THINK OF THEMSELVES AS CITIZENS WITH *RIGHTS* AND *DEMANDS*...

THE EMPIRE FALLS.

LEAVING IN ITS WAKE:

ARTIFICIALLY ADJUSTED BOUNDARIES

WHY DOES THAT ROCK HAVE PAINT ON IT?

ARTIFICIALLY MIXED POPULATIONS

THAT SURE IS A FUNNY OUTFIT YOU'RE WEARING...

FORMER IMPERIAL STOOGES AS RULERS

REMEMBER ME? I USED TO BE THE PROCURATOR!

NOT ADDING UP WELL IN THE PLUS COLUMN...

NOW I'M THE *SUPREME POTENTATE!*

SOMETIMES SMALLER POLITICAL UNITS EMERGE:

KINGDOM OF BOSNIA-12TH CENTURY C.E.

KINGDOM OF CROATIA-10TH CENTURY C.E.
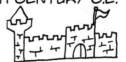

KINGDOM OF SERBIA-11TH CENTURY C.E.

KHANATE OF BULGARIA-9TH CENTURY C.E.

KINGDOM OF POLAND-10TH CENTURY C.E.

KINGDOM OF HUNGARY-10TH CENTURY C.E.

SOMETIMES ANOTHER EMPIRE COMES ALONG:

BUT THE MOST SERIOUS UPHEAVAL COMES FROM THE CONFLICT BETWEEN...

TWO EMPIRES
(OR SOMETIMES *MORE*)

FOR EXAMPLE, TAKE POLAND...

> **Note:** The authors wish to apologize for the inclusion of this cheap and tawdry Polish joke in an otherwise serious historical work with literary pretensions.

BUT SERIOUSLY:

IN THE 1700'S, POLAND, WHICH HAD BEEN A SOVEREIGN STATE SINCE 992 C.E., WAS DIVIDED UP BETWEEN RUSSIA, PRUSSIA, AND THE AUSTRO-HUNGARIAN EMPIRE.

WHAT HAD POLAND DONE TO DESERVE THIS SINGULAR FATE?

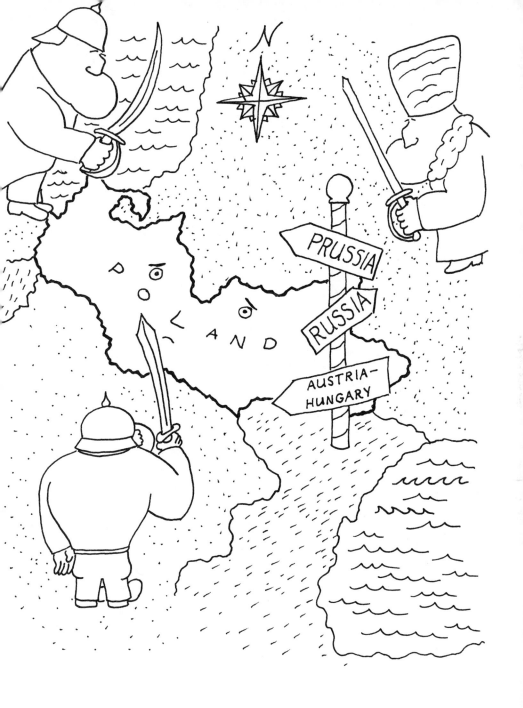

T HAPPENED TO OCCUPY A HUGE TRACT OF LAND
SMACK IN BETWEEN THREE EMPIRES, ALL OF WHOM
WERE ANXIOUS TO DO WHAT EMPIRES DO: *EXPAND*.

POLAND DISAPPEARED FROM THE MAP OF EUROPE
UNTIL 1918.

BULGARIA ALSO CHANGED SHAPE, SIZE, RELIGION, AND ETHNICITY MANY TIMES OVER THE AGES, SINCE IT WAS NESTLED COMFORTABLY BETWEEN THE BYZANTINE, OTTOMAN, RUSSIAN, AND AUSTRO-HUNGARIAN EMPIRES.

(BULGARIA DECLARED *ITSELF* AN EMPIRE FOR A WHILE IN 1186. THIS LASTED FOR 124 YEARS.)

...AND THEN THERE'S BOSNIA.

BOSNIA, PART OF THE ROMAN PROVINCE OF ILLYRICUM, WAS SETTLED BY SERBS IN THE 7TH CENTURY C.E.

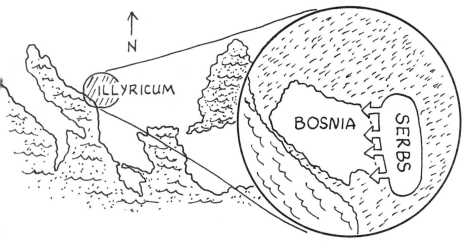

BUT IN 958, BOSNIA WAS RULED BY THE KING OF CROATIA

BETWEEN 1000 AND 1400, BOSNIA ALSO OCCASIONALY ACKNOWLEDGED THE OVERLORDSHIP OF HUNGARY.

IN THE 12TH CENTURY, BOSNIA DECLARED ITSELF A KINGDOM.

WHICH LASTED 200 YEARS, MEANWHILE ANNEXING HERZEGOVINA IN TO THE SOUTH...

...UNTIL 1463, WHEN THE KINGDOM OF BOSNIA FELL TO...

THE *TURKS* OF THE OTTOMAN EMPIRE—

WHO WERE ALSO CONQUERING SERBIA AND THE ENTIRE
ARAB EMPIRE FROM MOROCCO TO IRAQ.

THE TURKS WERE A PRESENCE IN THE REGION ALL THE
WAY UNTIL 1908.

IDELIGHT ON RELIGION AND ETHNICITY

THE CENTURIES OF OCCUPATION BY THE ANY BOSNIANS CONVERTED TO THE RELIGION OF THE OTTOMAN EMPIRE, BECOMING MUSLIM. THIS GAVE RISE TO A NEW, SLIGHTLY DIFFERENT ETHNIC GROUP, NEVER QUITE CATHOLIC/CROAT NOR QUITE ORTHODOX/SERB, BUT RATHER BOSNIAN MUSLIM, WITH SLIGHT DISTINCTIONS IN DRESS, CUISINE, DIALECT, AND FOLK TRADITIONS.

THE TURKS CLASSIFIED THEIR SUBJECT POPULATIONS BY RELIGION RATHER THAN NATIONAL BACKGROUND.

SINCE **SERBIA** WAS CLASSIFIED AS AN **ORTHODOX** COUNTRY, MOST **ORTHODOX BOSNIANS** BEGAN THINKING OF THEMSELVES AS **SERBS**. SINCE **CROATIA** WAS CLASSIFIED **CATHOLIC**, MOST **BOSNIAN CATHOLICS** CONSIDERED THEMSELVES **CROATIAN**. ONLY THE MUSLIMS IN BOSNIA ALWAYS CONSIDERED THEMSELVES **BOSNIAN**.

IN ACTUAL FACT, THE NATIONALITIES CONTINUED TO MIX AND BLEND TOGETHER, WITH DISTINCTIONS BECOMING LESS OBVIOUS AS TIME WENT ON. BOSNIA BECAME A MULTI-ETHNIC, MULTI-RELIGIOUS STATE, WITH RELIGIONS AND ETHNIC BACKGROUNDS OVERLAPPING, INTERTWINING, AND COEXISTING PEACEFULLY FOR SOME TIME.

MEANWHILE...

FOR 500 YEARS, THE OTTOMAN EMPIRE FOUGHT CON-
STANTLY OVER EASTERN EUROPE WITH THE HOLY RO-
MAN/HAPSBURG/AUSTRO-HUNGARIAN EMPIRE. AS THE
TWO EMPIRES FOUGHT, THE BOUNDARIES OF BOSNIA
KEPT CHANGING.

CROATIA AND SERBIA WERE BATTLEGROUNDS, TOO
WHEN THE TURKS WERE WINNING, THE BOUNDARIES OF
THE OTTOMAN EMPIRE MOVED AS FAR NORTH AS
CROATIA-

WHILE AT OTHER TIMES, CROATIA, BOSNIA, AND SERBIA WOULD ALL BE UNDER HAPSBURG/HOLY ROMAN RULE.

HAPSBURGS

☆ VIENNA

CROATIA

NORTH BOSNIA

• SARAJEVO

OTTOMAN EMPIRE

THIS WENT ON FOR 450 YEARS, REMEMBER, SO LOTS OF PEOPLE MOVED BACK AND FORTH TO DIFFERENT PLACES, TRYING TO KEEP OUT OF THE LINE OF BATTLE.

AND SOMETIMES *WHOLE VILLAGES* WERE *RELOCATED*, TO SERVE THE STRATEGIC NEEDS OF THE IMPERIAL ARMIES.

SO BY 1908, WHEN AUSTRIA-HUNGARY FINALLY ANNEXED BOSNIA AWAY FROM THE CRUMBLING OTTOMAN EMPIRE, THE POPULATION WAS SPREAD OUT LIKE...

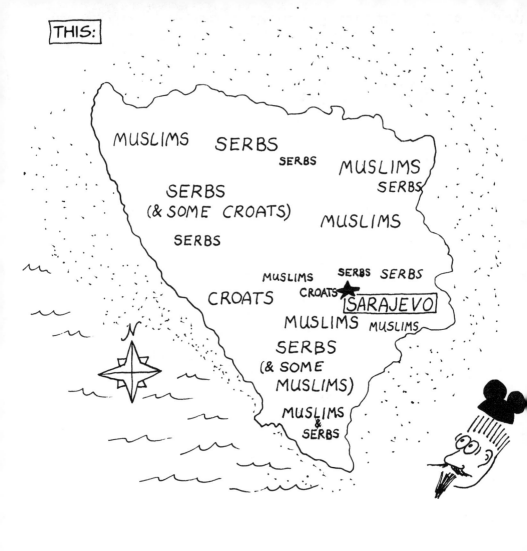

AND THEN **WORLD WAR ONE** CAME ALONG
-BUT WE'LL GET TO THAT LATER.

DOES ALL THIS BOUNDARY CHANGING AND RELOCATION HAVE ANY EFFECT ON THE LOCAL POPULACE?

DOES GOULASH HAVE PAPRIKA?

POLITICAL AWARENESS INCREASES...

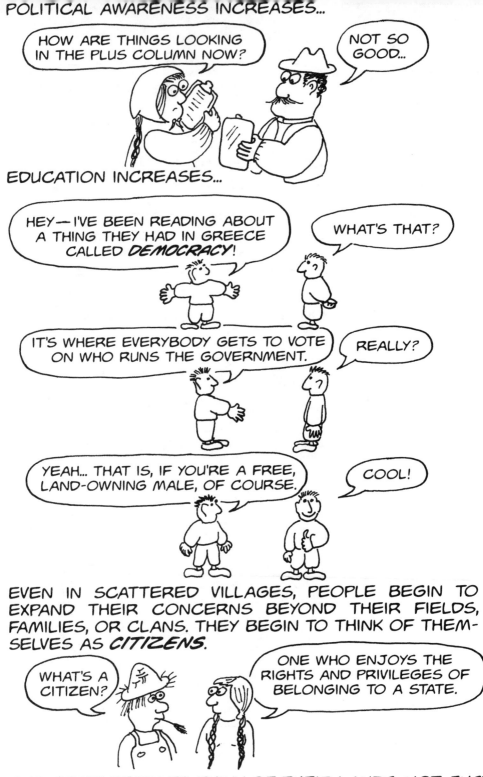

HOW ARE THINGS LOOKING IN THE PLUS COLUMN NOW?

NOT SO GOOD...

EDUCATION INCREASES...

HEY— I'VE BEEN READING ABOUT A THING THEY HAD IN GREECE CALLED *DEMOCRACY*!

WHAT'S THAT?

IT'S WHERE EVERYBODY GETS TO VOTE ON WHO RUNS THE GOVERNMENT.

REALLY?

YEAH... THAT IS, IF YOU'RE A FREE, LAND-OWNING MALE, OF COURSE.

COOL!

EVEN IN SCATTERED VILLAGES, PEOPLE BEGIN TO EXPAND THEIR CONCERNS BEYOND THEIR FIELDS, FAMILIES, OR CLANS. THEY BEGIN TO THINK OF THEM-SELVES AS *CITIZENS*.

WHAT'S A CITIZEN?

ONE WHO ENJOYS THE RIGHTS AND PRIVILEGES OF BELONGING TO A STATE.

AND SOME BEGIN TO THINK OF THEIR LANDS, NOT JUST AS PLACES, BUT AS...

CHAPTER FOUR

NATIONS

ACCORDING TO WEBSTER:

nation (nā´•shən), n. [from Latin *natio*, nation, race; orig. from Latin *natus*, being born] 1. A people connected by supposed ties of blood generally manifested by community of language, religion, customs, etc.

empire (ĕm´•pīr), n. [from Latin *imperium*, sovereignty] 1. A group of nations or states under a single sovereign power.

IN THE LATE 1700'S, POLITICAL PHILOSOPHERS BEGAN TO SPEAK OF *THE PEOPLE* AS A DRIVING FORCE IN HISTORY.

"MAN IS BORN FREE - AND EVERYWHERE HE IS IN CHAINS. ...THE GENERAL WILL ALONE CAN DIRECT THE STATE ACCORDING TO THE OBJECT FOR WHICH IT WAS INSTITUTED, I.E. THE COMMON GOOD..."

— Jean-Jacques Rousseau, *The Social Contract*

HEY - HE'S RIGHT!

YOU'RE RIGHT - HE'S RIGHT!

WE COULD RULE OURSELVES!

PEOPLE WERE GETTING TIRED OF EXISTING SOLELY AS PROPERTY OF MONARCHS AND EMPERORS - SO THE IDEA OF A STATE BASED ON THE SELF RULE AND SELF-DE-TERMINATION OF A PEOPLE - IN OTHER WORDS, A *NATION* - WAS BORN.

SO NATIONALISM STARTED OUT AS A REVOLUTIONARY, EGALITARIAN, POPULIST MOVEMENT?

YEP. TIMES CHANGE, DON'T THEY?

WITH THE *FRENCH REVOLUTION* OVERTURNING A MONARCHY, AND THE PRE-IMPERIAL NAPOLEON DEFEATING EMPIRES AND MONARCHIES RIGHT AND LEFT, THE *NATIONALIST* MOVEMENT SWEPT ACROSS EUROPE FROM FRANCE TO RUSSIA.

BUT HOW DO WE GET RID OF OUR MONARCHS?

THE SAME WAY THE FRENCH DID:

REVOLT!

(AND HOW DO EMPIRES RESPOND TO THIS?)

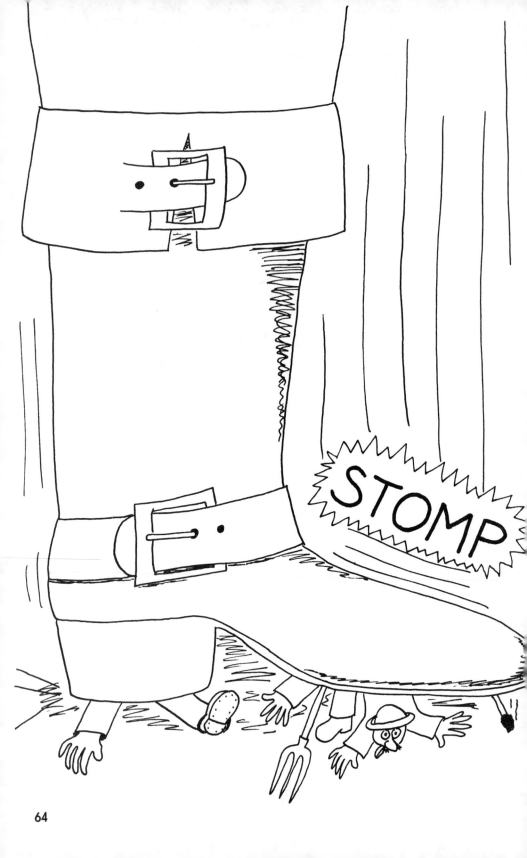

SOMETIMES IT WORKED...

GREECE
1821

SERBIA*
1817

*NOTE: AS SOON AS SERBIA BECAME A COUNTRY, SERBS STARTED DREAMING OF A *GREATER SERBIA*. WE'LL HEAR MORE ABOUT THAT LATER.

HUNGARY
1848

BOHEMIA
1848

SERBIA AGAIN
1867

BOSNIA
1875

AND, OF COURSE, OUR REVOLUTION IN FRANCE WAS A GREAT SUCCESS!

WELL, SURE - THOUGH FRANCE WAS AN EMPIRE AGAIN IN 20 YEARS...

...AND SOMETIMES IT *DIDN'T* WORK.

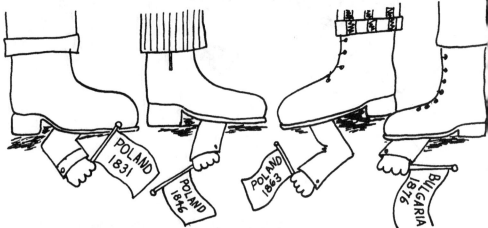

(MAINLY BECAUSE, AFTER THE FINAL DEFEAT OF NAPO-
LEON IN 1815, THE THREE IMPERIAL MONARCHS OF
RUSSIA, PRUSSIA, AND *AUSTRIA* UNITED TO FORM A
"HOLY ALLIANCE" AGAINST ALL THE NATIONALIST UPRIS-
INGS IN THEIR DOMINIONS.)

THE BATTLE - BETWEEN **POPULIST NATIONALISM** ON THE LEFT AND **REACTIONARY CONSERVATIVE IMPE- RIALISM** ON THE RIGHT - CONTINUED THROUGHOUT THE '800'S AND WELL INTO THE 20TH CENTURY.

NOT THAT NATIONALISM DOESN'T HAVE ITS DRAWBACKS, TOO.

LIKE WHAT?

FOR ONE THING, AS TOYNBEE SAYS -

"THE DESTRUCTIVENESS OF NATIONALISM IS PRO- PORTIONATE TO THE DEGREE OF THE DISCRPANCY BETWEEN THE IDEAL OF NATIONALISM AND THE LOCAL STATE OF EXISTING GEOGRAPHICAL AND POLITICAL FACTS."

Arnold Toynbee. *A Study of History.*
London: Oxford University Press, 1954

WHAT'S THAT MEAN?

HE MEANS THAT THE ACTUAL "IDEAL OF NATION- ALISM" IS **ONE HOMOGENOUS ETHNIC GROUP PER NATION,** BUT SINCE GEOGRAPHICAL AND POLITICAL BORDERS RARELY SHAKE DOWN THAT WAY - ESPECIALLY IN EASTERN EUROPE - NATION- ALISM USUALLY ENDS UP WITH **ONE ETHNIC GROUP RULING OVER OTHERS.**

OH.

THIS LEADS TO CONFLICT AND EVEN **ETHNIC CLEANSING -** BUT WE'LL GET TO THAT LATER. FURTHERMORE, EVEN RULING ETHNIC GROUPS ARE OFTEN DOMINATED BY UPPER-CLASS MINORITIES.

OH.

FURTHERMORE...

WELL AT LEAST WE'RE NOT RULED BY TURKS.

SO THROUGHOUT THE 19TH AND 20TH CENTURIES, TWO KINDS OF CONFLICT WERE GOING ON...

NATION VS. EMPIRE

AND

EMPIRE VS. EMPIRE

BY THE BEGINNING OF THE 20TH CENTURY, THE EMPIRES OF EUROPE WERE STRUGGLING FOR CONTROL OF MOST OF THE KNOWN WORLD.

THE RESULT?

CHAPTER FIVE

WORLD WAR ONE

HOT DOGS! CRACKER JACKS!

GETCHER PROGRAM FOR THE WAR TO END ALL WARS!

GETCHER PROGRAM! CAN'T TELL THE PLAYERS WITHOUT A PROGRAM!

WWI
SCORECARD
Mobilizations and declarations of war

Player	vs.	Date
Austria-Hungary	Serbia	July 28, 1914
Russia	Austria-Hungary	July 30, 1914
Germany	Russia	Aug. 1, 1914
Great Britain	Germany	Aug. 4, 1914
Austria-Hungary	Russia	Aug. 5, 1914
Serbia	Germany	Aug. 6, 1914
Montenegro	Austria-Hungary	Aug. 7, 1914
Montenegro	Germany	Aug. 12, 1914
France	Austria-Hungary	Aug. 10, 1914
Great Britain	Austria-Hungary	Aug. 12, 1914
Japan	Germany	Aug. 23, 1914
Austria-Hungary	Japan	Aug. 25, 1914
Austria-Hungary	Belgium	Aug. 28, 1914
Russia	Turkey	Nov. 1, 1914
Great Britain & France	Turkey	Nov. 3, 1914
Italy	Austria-Hungary	May 23, 1915
Bulgaria	Serbia	Oct. 11, 1915
Romania	Austria-Hungary	Aug. 27, 1916
Germany	Romania	Aug. 28, 1916
Turkey	Romania	Aug. 30, 1916
Bulgaria	Romania	Sept. 1, 1916
Greece	Germany & Bulgaria	Nov. 27, 1916
U.S.A.	Germany	April 6, 1917
China	Germany & Austria-Hungary	Aug. 14, 1917
Cuba, Panama, Haiti, Brazil, Guatamala, Nicaragua, Costa Rica & Honduras	Germany	July, 1918

BY 1914, THE **EMPIRES** OF RUSSIA, PRUSSIA, AUSTRIA-HUNGARY, AND OTTOMAN TURKEY HAD BEEN FIGHTING **WITH** AND **AGAINST** EACH OTHER IN DIFFERENT COMBINATIONS FOR 500 YEARS - AND **ESPECIALLY** THE LAST FIFTY - MEANWHILE RESISTING THE EFFORTS OF POLES, CZECHS, ROMANIANS, SERBS, CROATS, BULGARIANS, AND BOSNIANS TO GAIN INDEPENDENCE.

IN 1914, THEREFORE, THE MAP LOOKED LIKE THIS:

...OR, IN GRAPHIC TERMS, LIKE THIS:

WITH ALL THESE EMPIRES RUNNING OUT OF NEW LANDS AND PEOPLES TO CONQUER AND EXPLOIT FOR TAXES, RESOURCES, AND SOLDIERS, THE EMPIRES TURNED ON EACH OTHER.

THREATS ENSUED.

ALL IT TOOK WAS ONE LITTLE MATCH, AND...

G. PRINCIP

IN 1908, AUSTRIA-HUNGARY ANNEXED SLOVENIA AND
BOSNIA. ON JUNE 28, 1914, IN SARAJEVO IN BOSNIA, A
YOUNG ANARCHIST NAMED GAVRILO PRINCIP SHOT AND
KILLED THE ARCHDUKE FRANZ FERDINAND, HEIR TO THE
AUSTRO-HUNGARIAN IMPERIAL THRONE, AND HIS WIFE.
    AUSTRIA INSISTED THAT THE ASSASSIN WAS A SERB;
SERBIA INSISTED HE WAS BOSNIAN, BUT AUSTRIA DE-
CLARED WAR ON SERBIA ANYWAY. RUSSIA WAS ALLIED
WITH SERBIA; FRANCE WAS ALLIED WITH RUSSIA; GER-
MANY WAS ALLIED WITH AUSTRIA-HUNGARY; GERMANY
MARCHED THROUGH BELGIUM, WHICH WAS ALLIED WITH
GREAT BRITAIN, AND BEFORE YOU KNOW IT...

THE WAR TO END ALL WARS

AS A RESULT OF THE WAR:

THE OTTOMAN EMPIRE FELL

THE RUSSIAN EMPIRE FELL (TAKEN OVER BY BOLSHEVIKS)

THE AUSTRO-HUNGARIAN EMPIRE FELL

THE GERMAN EMPIRE FELL (FOR A WHILE)

FRANCE GOT KNOCKED FOR A LOOP

BOHEMIA, MORAVIA, SILESIA, AND SLOVAKIA UNITED THEMSELVES INTO CZECHOSLOVAKIA

POLAND DECLARED ITSELF INDEPEN-DENT

HUNGARY BECAME INDEPENDENT

BULGARIA, ROMANIA, AND GREECE MAINTAINED INDEPENDENCE

SERBIA, CROATIA, AND SLOVENIA UNITED INTO THE SERB-CROAT-SLOVENE STATE

WHY WASN'T BOSNIA INCLUDED?

BECAUSE WHEN AUSTRIA-HUNGARY FELL, SERBIA ANNEXED BOSNIA, DE-CLARING THAT BOSNIANS WERE RE-ALLY SERBS ANYWAY. REMEMBER THE DREAMS OF GREATER SERBIA?

SO BOSNIA DISAPPEARED?

FOR ABOUT 30 YEARS.

SO IN 1919, THE MAP LOOKED LIKE...

CHAPTER SIX

BETWEEN THE WARS

AFTER THE WAR, EUROPE WAS DIVIDED INTO NATIONS...

FOR ONE THING, MUCH OF EUROPE LOOKED LIKE THIS.

- A WHOLE GENERATION OF MALES HAD BEEN KILLED.

- NATURAL RESOURCES HAD BEEN DESTROYED.

- THE ECONOMIES OF EVERY COUNTRY IN EUROPE WERE IN SHAMBLES.

AND THE WORLD-WIDE DEPRESSION HADN'T EVEN STARTED YET!

FURTHERMORE, THE POWERS-THAT-WERE AT VERSAILLES DID NOT ALWAYS DISTRIBUTE LAND OR CREATE BORDERS IN THE MOST EQUITABLE, JUST, OR FAR-SEEING MANNER.

WILSON

LLOYD GEORGE

CLEMENCEAU

ORLANDO

JUST LOOK WHAT THEY DID TO THE MIDDLE EAST... BUT *DON'T GET ME STARTED*!

FOR EXAMPLE, *GERMANY* WAS NOT ONLY DEPRIVED OF ALL ITS IMPERIAL HOLDINGS BY THE TREATY OF VERSAILLES, BUT WAS ALSO REDUCED TO ABJECT POVERTY AND SHACKLED WITH AN ASTRONOMICAL WAR REPARATIONS DEBT WHICH IT HAD NO MEANS TO PAY.

GRRR!

CONFLICT RESOLUTION DEVICE

THE MOSTLY-DEMOCRATIC GOVERNMENTS LEFT IN POWER WERE FACED WITH THE IMPOSSIBLE TASK OF SORTING OUT ALL THESE INTERLOCKING MESSES...

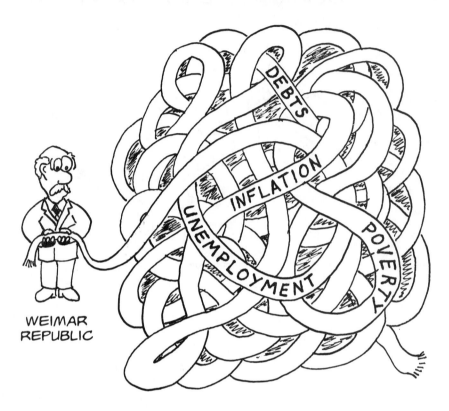

WEIMAR REPUBLIC

...AND MOSTLY THEY FAILED.

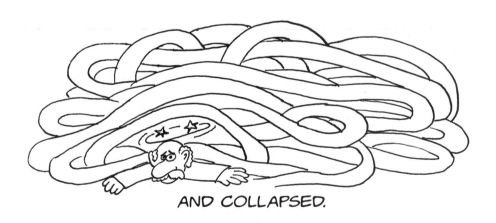

AND COLLAPSED.

DISCONTENT AND ANGER WERE EVERYWHERE, WHICH GAVE RISE TO VARIOUS EXTREMIST POLITICAL FACTIONS.

IF YOU ASKED KARL MARX, HE WOULD HAVE SAID SOMETHING LIKE...

COMMUNISM IS THE ULTIMATE STATE, WHEREIN ALL FACTORIES AND ALL MEANS OF PRODUCTION ARE OWNED COLLECTIVELY BY ALL PEOPLE.

SOCIALISM, ON THE OTHER HAND, IS AN INTERMEDIATE STATE WHEREIN THE DICTATORSHIP BY THE PROLETARIAN WORKING CLASS BRINGS ABOUT GOVERNMENT OWNERSHIP OF THE MEANS OF PRODUCTION.

ONLY HE WOULD'VE SAID IT IN GERMAN

IN OUR CENTURY, *COMMUNISM* HAS COME TO MEAN THE DICTATORSHIP OF THE COMMUNIST PARTY, AND *SOCIALISM* HAS COME TO REFER TO ANY GOVERNMENT WHICH REGULATES INDUSTRY, IN WHOLE OR PART, AND IS HEAVILY INVOLVED IN SOCIAL PROGRAMS.

ON THE OTHER HAND, TO MANY PEOPLE COMMUNISM AND SOCIALISM HAVE ALWAYS MEANT THE SAME THING...

SO THE WESTERN POWERS NEVER SUPPORTED THE LEFT WING SOCIALIST/COMMUNIST MOVEMENTS—ESPE- CIALLY THE BOLSHEVIK COMMUNISTS, WHO IN 1917 TOOK OVER RUSSIA AND TRANSFORMED THE OLD EMPIRE INTO THE **U**NION OF **S**OVIET **S**OCIALIST **R**EPUBLICS.

ЛЕНИН

THIS MAN WILL EAT YOUR CHIL- DREN, DRINK YOUR BLOOD, AND PUT YOU OUT OF A JOB!!

AFTER THE DEATH OF LENIN IN 1924, THE U.S.S.R. OBLIGED ITS CAPITALIST DETRACTORS BY SUP- PLANTING THE TRUE COMMUNIST SYSTEM WITH A ONE-PARTY ELITE GOVERNMENT WHICH BECAME INCREASINGLY TOTALITARIAN UNDER <u>JOSEF STALIN</u>. WE'LL BE SEEING MORE OF HIM.

WELL, IF WE CAN'T HAVE SOCIALISM, WHAT'S LEFT?

THE **OPPOSITE** EXTREME REACTION TO SOCIAL AND ECONOMIC CHAOS WAS...

WE ARE THE BEST! WE HAVE ALWAYS BEEN THE BEST! ALL OF OUR TROUBLES ARE CAUSED BY *THEM*!

WHO'S "*THEM*"?

YOU PICK.

NATIONALISM IN THE EXTREME, OR...

HYPERNATIONALISM

NATIONALIST PRIDE BECAME AN EXCUSE FOR RACISM AND FASCISM. SINCE THE RULING CLASSES WERE AFRAID OF COMMUNISM, THEY TENDED TO SUPPORT HARMLESS RIGHT WING EXTREMISTS LIKE BENITO MUSSOLINI AND ADOLF HITLER.

AS A RESULT, ONE BY ONE, MOST OF THE COUNTRIES OF EUROPE BECAME FASCIST.

HUNGARY	1919
ITALY	1922
ROMANIA	1930
GERMANY	1933
YUGOSLAVIA	1934
CROATIA	1942
SPAIN	1939

WELL, AT LEAST THEY'RE NOT COMMUNIST!

HYPERNATIONALISTS LIKE HITLER AND MUSSOLINI NOT ONLY NATIONALIZED THEIR POPULACE, BUT NATIONALIZED THEIR INDUSTRIES AS WELL.

BUT THAT SOUNDS LIKE SOCIALISM!

YEAH, SO WHAT?

HITLER'S PARTY IN GERMANY WAS ACTUALLY CALLED THE *NATIONAL SOCIALIST GERMAN WORKERS' PARTY,* WHICH WAS ABBREVIATED IN GERMAN *NSDAP*, OR *NAZI.*

SEE? THE BEST OF BOTH WORLDS. GOVERNMENT REGULATED INDUSTRY, *AND* THE TRAINS RUN ON TIME! PLUS PLENTY OF ETHNIC FOREIGNERS TO BLAME ANY PROBLEMS ON!

HITLER WAS SO SUCCESSFUL IN GERMANY — AND MUSSOLINI IN ITALY — THAT SOON THEY ROUSED PUBLIC SUPPORT FOR APPLYING THEIR NATIONALISM TO *OTHER NATIONS.*

HEY - THERE ARE *GERMANS* BEING *OPPRESSED* OVER THERE IN *AUSTRIA*!

AND ALSO IN CZECHOSLOVAKIA!

(ANNEXED 1938)

AND WHAT ABOUT POLAND?!

(ANNEXED 1939)

ALBANIA HAS ANCESTRAL RELATIONS WITH ITALY!

(ANNEXED 1939)

AND AREN'T THOSE *ITALIANS* IN *ETHIOPIA*?

(CONQUERED BACK IN 1936)

SPOTLIGHT ON YUGOSLAVIA

BOTH GERMANY AND ITALY HAD DESIGNS ON YUGOSLAVIA

AFTER OCCUPYING ALBANIA, MUSSOLINI SENT PRO-FASCIST ALBANIANS TO INFILTRATE KOSOVO IN SOUTHERN YUGOSLAVIA, PREPARING FOR AN INVASION IN 1941.

HITLER INVADED CROATIA, BOSNIA, AND SERBIA IN 1941. THE NAZI PUPPET GOVERNMENT IN CROATIA WAS PARTICULARLY NASTY, PERSECUTING AND SLAUGHTERING SERBS (AND JEWS AND GYPSIES), SOME OF WHOSE FAMILIES HAD LIVED THERE FOR HUNDREDS OF YEARS.

THINGS ARE LOOKING UP!

...AND FINALLY THESE TWO HYPERNATIONALISTS, ALONG WITH ONE OLD FASHIONED IMPERIALIST, WERE REVIVING OLD TRADITIONS.

BUT, SINCE THE WESTERN CAPITALIST EMPIRES WEREN'T GOING TO STAND FOR THIS...

AND SO, WE WERE LED INTO...

CHAPTER SEVEN

WORLD WAR ~~ONE~~ TWO

BLAM

GERMANY, ITALY, AND JAPAN WERE DEFEATED IN 1945.

THE *RUSSIANS* ATTACKED FROM THE *EAST*; THE *U.S.* AND *ENGLAND* ATTACKED FROM THE *WEST*; RESISTANCE FIGHTERS IN *YUGOSLAVIA*, LED BY A YOUNG SOCIALIST NAMED *TITO*, FREED YUGOSLAVIA WITHOUT ANY HELP FROM THE ALLIES.

AND WHAT DID THE 2.5 GOOD GUYS DO?

"WE RID THE WORLD OF THE FASCIST MENACE!"

HERE'S HOW THINGS SHOOK DOWN:

GERMANY WAS SPLIT IN HALF.

GRRR!

ENGLAND, HAVING LOST MOST OF ITS IMPERIAL POSSESSIONS, BECAME A SINGLE, SMALL CAPITALIST NATION.

UNCLE SAM OCCUPIED MOST OF WESTERN EUROPE.

AND THE USSR OCCUPIED MOST OF EASTERN EUROPE, EITHER WITH SOLDIERS OR WITH PUPPET GOVERNMENTS.

KEY:

SAM   ★★★

IVAN   ♩♩♩

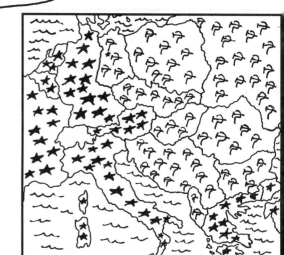

IN THE FOLLOWING YEARS, UNCLE SAM AND IVAN THE BEAR HAD LITTLE GOOD TO SAY ABOUT EACH OTHER.

THEY EAT BABIES!

THEY STEAL FROM THE MOUTHS OF WORKERS!

IN THE UNITED STATES, **WE** WERE TAUGHT:

U.S. = FREEDOM

U.S.S.R. = SLAVERY

IN THE SOVIET UNION, **THEY** WERE TAUGHT:

U.S.S.R. = FREEDOM, EQUALITY

U.S. = CAPITALIST SLAVERY

IN TRUTH, SAM AND IVAN WERE REALLY NOTHING BUT TWO DIFFERENT KINDS OF...

THE TWO EMPIRES, HOWEVER, HAD VERY DIFFERENT STYLES...

THE SOVIETS, HAVING BEEN INVADED TWICE WITHIN 150 YEARS, WERE CONCERNED WITH SECURE BORDERS.

A MILLION DIED WHEN NAPOLEON INVADED IN 1812.

15 MILLION DIED WHEN HITLER INVADED IN 1943.

THE SECURITY ZONE CONSISTED OF CZECHOSLOVAKIA, POLAND, EAST GERMANY, HUNGARY, ROMANIA, BULGARIA, ALBANIA, AND, TO A LESSER EXTENT, YUGOSLAVIA.

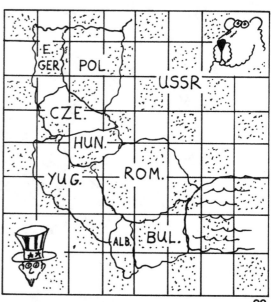

UNCLE SAM PLAYED THE GAME DIFFERENTLY.

THE UNITED STATES

    A) HASN'T BEEN INVADED SINCE 1812, AND

    B) IS CONCERNED WITH ECONOMIC DOMINA-
    TION MORE THAN POLITICAL CONTROL.

SO, INSTEAD OF PLAYING "SECURE BORDERS" THE U.S. PLAYED *WORLDWIDE LEAPFROG AND ENCIRCLE-MENT.*

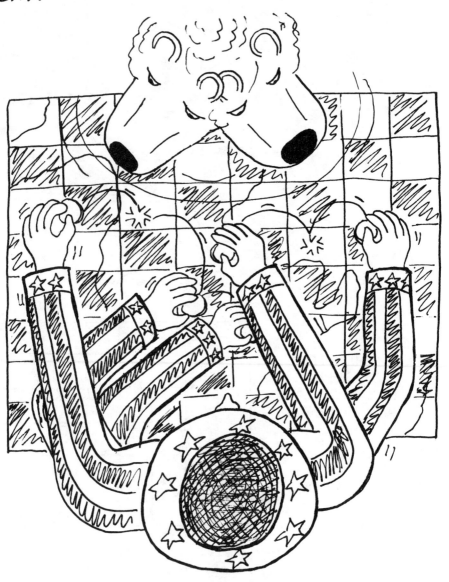

THE UNITED STATES UPPED THE ANTE BY ADDING NEW INNOVATIONS TO THE GAME:

THE SOVIETS SOON LEARNED TO PLAY WITH THE SAME GAME PIECES...

...AND FURTHERMORE INTRODUCED ANOTHER INNOVATION:

CHAPTER EIGHT

THE COMMUNIST YEARS

AFTER WORLD WAR TWO, WHEN EASTERN EUROPE FELL UNDER THE SOVIET "SPHERE OF INFLUENCE", THE U.S.S.R. DID NOT ACTUALLY ANNEX THESE COUNTRIES.

INSTEAD, THE NATIONS OF EASTERN EUROPE BECAME PART OF THE WORLD INTERNATIONAL COMMUNIST FRONT —IN PART BECAUSE MANY EASTERN EUROPEANS WERE GENUINELY COMMITTED TO THE ORIGINAL MARXIST-COMMUNIST IDEALS...

> EVERYBODY WORKS, NO-BODY STARVES, RIGHT?

...AND IN PART BECAUSE OF TRADE AGREEMENTS WHEREBY THE U.S.S.R. SOLD RAW MATERIALS DIRT CHEAP TO SMALLER NATIONS IN RETURN FOR POLITICAL OBEDIENCE.

THUS, STALIN AND THE SOVIET GOVERNMENT WERE ABLE TO IMPLEMENT PROGRAMS THROUGH LOCAL GOVERN-MENTS WHICH, THOUGH INDEPENDENT, BECAME IN EF-FECT...

PUPPETS, A.K.A. SATELLITES

ALL OF THESE SATELLITE COUNTRIES WERE PARLIA-
MENTARY DEMOCRACIES - NOMINALLY, AT LEAST.

THEY HAD CONSTITUTIONS...

CONSTITUTION

ARTICLE I: The Party is the Boss.

ARTICLE II: No other parties are allowed.

ARTICLE III: The U.S.S.R. is our Motherland and Father-land.

ARTICLE IV: No crossing against red lights.

AND PARLIAMENTS...

AND ELECTIONS.

VOTE COMMUNIST

IF YOU WANT TO KEEP LIVING HERE

SEVERAL OF THESE COUNTRIES WERE EXTREMELY **POOR** TO BEGIN WITH.

I'M NOT AS POOR AS THESE GUYS- I'VE GOT A HAT!

ALBANIA

ROMANIA

BULGARIA

STALIN HOPED TO IMPROVE THE ECONOMIES OF THESE COUNTRIES BY BUILDING LOTS OF HEAVY INDUSTRIES, USING MONEY GENERATED BY IMPROVED, COLLECTIV- IZED AGRICULTURE.

HIS PROGRAM OF COLLECTIVIZATION, HOWEVER, MERELY LED TO WIDESPREAD DISCONTENT...

BASTARDS TOOK MY FARM AWAY!

SUPPOSE THEY THINK I'M GONNA BUST MY BUTT ON THEIR COLLECTIVE FARM? HAH!

...AND STILL FAILED TO GENERATE ENOUGH REVENUE FOR HIS PROGRAM OF HEAVY INDUSTRIALIZATION...

CAIN'T GET NO SOVIET BLOOD FROM NO ALBANIAN TURNIP!

...WHICH FORCED COUNTRIES LIKE ALBANIA AND ROMANIA TO BORROW HEAVILY — OFTEN FROM WESTERN COUN- TRIES.

ER...THANKS.

IN FAIRNESS, STALINISM ACTUALLY IMPROVED THE STANDARD OF LIVING IN SOME COUNTRIES.

FOR EXAMPLE, IN ROCKY, POVERTY-STRICKEN ALBANIA SOME PEOPLE FELT...

WE WAS DIRT POOR BEFORE *PAPA JOE* CAME ALONG AND INVESTED *BUSHELS* O' CORN INTO AGRICULTURE AND HEAVY INDUSTRY. HE COLLECTIVIZED ALL OUR LITTLE GOOD-FOR-NOTHIN' FARMS INTO BIG FARMING UNITS, SO'S WE COULD AFFORD FARM MACHINERY 'N' SUCH. *BEFORE*, ALL WE HAD WAS HOES AND PICKS. *NOW*, WE GOT...

INDUSTRY!

PA-CHING!

JOBS!

TRACTORS!

THERE WERE SIMILAR STORIES IN ROMANIA AND BULGARIA.

INCIDENTALLY, ALL THIS MECHANIZATION GAVE STALIN GREATER CONTROL OVER THE POPULATIONS. "GENGHIS KHAN WITH A TELEPHONE" HE WAS CALLED.

106

WE WERE JUST *FINE*! OUR *FARMLAND* WAS *GOOD*, AND OUR *ECONOMIES* WERE *RECOVERING*! WE HAD PRIVATE INDUSTRIES. AND THEN *STALIN* CAME ALONG AND *COLLECTIVIZED* EVERYTHING. INSTEAD OF CONSUMER GOODS, ALL OF A SUDDEN WE WERE FLOODED WITH *TRACTORS* AND *BRIDGES* AND *STATUES* OF PEOPLE WITH SLEDGE HAMMERS. NOW EVERYTHING IS ALL *MESSED UP* ...

WHAT?

CLICK

NOTHING.

SPOTLIGHT ON YUGOSLAVIA

IN THE SERB-CROAT-SLOVENE STATE, WHICH CHANGED ITS NAME TO *YUGOSLAVIA* IN 1929, THE GERMANS WERE KICKED OUT, NOT BY THE U.S. OR U.S.S.R., BUT BY RESISTANCE ARMIES LED BY A YOUNG MARSHAL NAMED *JOSIP BROZ*, WHO TOOK THE NAME *TITO*.

THUS, AT THE END OF THE WAR, YUGOSLAVIA WAS OCCUPIED BY *ITSELF*. TITO HAD THE SERBIAN KING DEPOSED AND BECAME PREMIER OF THE *PEOPLE'S REPUBLIC OF YUGOSLAVIA*, MADE UP OF SIX CONSTITUENT STATES: SERBIA, CROATIA, SLOVENIA, BOSNIA-HERZEGOVINA, MACEDONIA, AND MONTENEGRO.

NOTE THAT WHILE BOSNIA WAS DESIGNATED AN AUTONOMOUS REGION, THE BOSNIAN MUSLIMS WERE NOT CONSIDERED ONE OF THE "CONSTITUENT PEOPLES" OF YUGOSLAVIA. THIS WAS BECAUSE TITO—GOOD COMMUNIST THAT HE WAS — DID NOT RECOGNIZE *ANY RELIGION* OR RELIGIOUS DISTINCTION. SO EVERYONE IN BOSNIA WAS FORCED TO REGISTER AS SERB, CROAT, OR OTHER.

THESE RULES WERE RELAXED SOMEWHAT AFTER 20 YEARS. IN THE 1971 CENSUS, BOSNIAN MUSLIMS WERE ALLOWED TO REGISTER AS "MUSLIM".

TITO WAS A COMMUNIST, AND YUGOSLAVIA WAS PART OF THE WORLD INTERNATIONAL COMMUNIST FRONT, BUT TITO REMAINED INDEPENDENT OF STALIN'S DIRECT CONTROL. HE THEREFORE COLLECTIVIZED SOME FARMS AND INDUSTRIES, BUT HE ALSO ALLOWED SOME PRIVATE INDUSTRY AND FARMING.

TITO WAS ABLE TO WALK A FINE LINE BETWEEN THE WESTERN AND EASTERN POWERS, WHICH ENABLED HIM TO BORROW MONEY FROM THE WEST - WHICH SEEMED LIKE A GOOD IDEA AT THE TIME.

TITO'S REIGN LASTED UNTIL HE DIED IN 1980. IMMEDIATELY THEREAFTER, TENSIONS AROSE BETWEEN CROATS, SLOVENES, BOSNIANS, AND THE DOMINANT SERBS, WHO STILL WANTED TO CREATE A *GREATER SERBIA*.

IN 1953, JOSEF STALIN DIED.

SOME OF THE EASTERN BLOC COUNTRIES THOUGHT
THIS WOULD MEAN A LOOSENING OF THE U.S.S.R.'S IRON
CONTROL.

HUNGARY 1956

THEY WERE WRONG.

...HOWEVER, WITH NIKITA KRUSHCHEV'S "DE-STALINIZATION" PROGRAM...

STALIN DID MANY *BAD* THINGS.

...THERE WAS *SOME* RELAXATION OF SOVIET CONTROL...

...AS LONG AS YOU DIDN'T GET *TOO* RELAXED:

CZECHOSLOVAKIA 1968

NONETHELESS, KRUSHCHEV'S ATTEMPTED REFORMS BEGAN A PROCESS WHICH GORBACHEV WOULD CONTINUE 30 YEARS LATER.

THERE WERE MANY ATTEMPTS AT REFORM AND LIBER-
ALIZATION IN THE U.S.S.R., BUT THEY ALWAYS CAME UP
AGAINST THE LEGACY OF STALIN:

THE PARTY LEADER-
SHIP KNOWS BEST!

WITH THE DICTATORSHIP OF THE PARTY REPLACING
MARX'S DICTATORSHIP OF THE PROLETARIAT, MEMBERS
OF THE PARTY LEADERSHIP WERE IN ABSOLUTE CON-
TROL. THIS OF COURSE LED TO EXCESS AND CORRUP-
TION...

IT IS IN THE BEST
INTEREST OF THE
PARTY THAT I BE
DRIVEN AROUND IN
A LIMOUSINE!

...NOT ONLY IN THE U.S.S.R. BUT IN EASTERN BLOC
COUNTRIES AS WELL. FOR EXAMPLE...

IN *ROMANIA*, SECRETARY GENERAL *NICOLAE CEAUSESCU* – WHO WAS ALSO PRESIDENT, CHAIRMAN OF THE NATIONAL DEFENSE COUNCIL, SUPREME COMMANDER OF THE ARMED FORCES, AND CHAIRMAN OF A BUNCH OF OTHER THINGS – FILLED GOVERNMENT POSTS WITH MEMBERS OF HIS OWN FAMILY...

ROMANIAN GOVERNMENT

WIFE	BROTHER		BROTHER	BROTHER	SON	
ELENA					NICU	

..OUTLAWED ANY NUMBER OF CHILDREN GREATER THAN TWO – THEN TOOK THE EXCESS CHILDREN AND RAISED THEM AS HIS PERSONAL BODYGUARDS.

HIS GRANDIOSE BUILDING SCHEMES AND FAILED INDUSTRIES LEFT THE PEOPLE OF ROMANIA LITERALLY STARVING TO DEATH FOR 20 YEARS, WHILE CEAUSESCU CONTINUED DECORATING BUCHAREST AND FILLING THE COUNTRY WITH STATUES OF HIMSELF.

MEANWHILE, IN THE *WEST*...

THE WESTERN COUNTRIES WERE DOMINATED BY CAPITALISM, WHICH, ALTHOUGH IT PRODUCES *POVERTY*, *UNEMPLOYMENT*, AND A *HUGE GAP BETWEEN RICH AND POOR*, ALSO PRODUCES LOTS OF...

STUFF!

...EVEN IF MANY CAN'T AFFORD IT.

W. E.

WE WANT CALVIN KLEIN

SO THE RISING DISCONTENT IN EASTERN BLOC COUNTRIES WAS NOT BECAUSE THEY ENVIED OUR FREEDOM?

NOPE. WHAT THEY ENVIED WAS OUR *STUFF*.

ECONOMIC GROWTH COMPARISONS LOOKED LIKE THIS:

IN SOVIET-BLOC COUNTRIES, THE STATE PROVIDED EDUCATION, HEALTH CARE, TRANSPORTATION, JOBS, AND HOUSING - BUT LITTLE CHOICE AND FEW LUXURIES. THE STORES WERE CHRONICALLY SHORT OF **CONSUMER GOODS**.

THE COMMUNIST GOVERNMENTS (INCLUDING TITO'S IN YUGOSLAVIA) KEPT MAKING PROMISES THAT THEY COULDN'T KEEP.

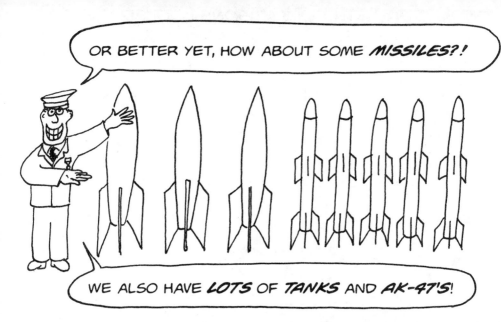

MEANWHILE, **MASSIVE MILITARY SPENDING** WAS **DRAINING** THE **ECONOMIES** OF THE U.S.S.R. AND MOST OF ITS SATELLITE NATIONS, CREATING HUGE DEBTS.

SOME COUNTRIES, SUCH AS POLAND AND HUNGARY, TRIED TO GET OUT OF DEBT BY BORROWING HEAVILY FROM WESTERN COUNTRIES.

Y 1980, CITIZENS OF THE WORLD INTERNATIONAL COM-
UNIST FRONT WERE REACHING THEIR LIMITS.

OMANIA WAS SIMMERING.

OLISH WORKERS WERE BOILING.

TO WAS DEAD, AND THE GOVERNMENT OF YUGOSLAVIA
AS DECENTRALIZED, CAUSING TROUBLE BETWEEN
LOVENIA, WHICH WANTED AUTONOMY, AND SERBIA,
HICH WANTED A STRONGER, CENTRALIZED STATE, WITH
ERBS IN CHARGE.

ND WESTERN ADVERTISING HAD MADE INROADS INTO
OST COUNTRIES:

SOMETHING WAS BOUND TO HAPPEN.

CHAPTER NINE

THE CHESSBOARD CRACKS

IN 1980, SHIPYARD WORKERS IN GDANSK, POLAND, STRIKE FOR HIGHER WAGES.

- *1980* - THE MOVEMENT FOR BETTER WAGES AND CONDITIONS SPREADS ACROSS POLAND, NAMING ITSELF WITH AN OLD COMMUNIST TERM: *SOLIDARITY*.

- *1981* - THE POLISH GOVERNMENT DECLARES MARTIAL LAW.

NOTE THAT THE *U.S.S.R.* STAYED OUT OF IT, SINCE IT WASN'T THE POLISH *GOVERNMENT* THAT WAS DISSENTING, BUT MERELY *CITIZENS* DISSENTING AGAINST THE GOVERNMENT.

- *1982* - THE POLISH GOVERNMENT BANS THE SOLIDARITY MOVEMENT.

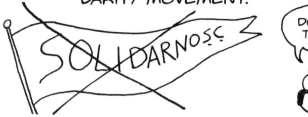

SOLIDARITY STAYS BANNED UNTIL 1989.

BUT MEANWHILE...

IN THE U.S.S.R.:

1985 - **MIKHAIL GORBACHEV** COMES TO POWER AS **PREMIER** AND **HEAD OF THE COMMUNIST PARTY**. HE PERCEIVES THAT THE U.S.S.R. WILL CRUMBLE WITHOUT REFORM.

THINGS MUST CHANGE!

1986 - GORBACHEV IMPLEMENTS **GLASNOST** ("OPENNESS"), MEANING A **MORE OPEN SOCIETY**.

LET'S TALK!

1987 - HE IMPLEMENTS **PERESTROIKA** ("RESTRUCTURING"), MEANING THAT **OTHER POLITICAL PARTIES** WILL BE ALLOWED INTO THE SYSTEM, AND COMMUNIST SOCIETY AND ECONOMY WILL BE **REFORMED**.

GRADUALLY AND WITHIN LIMITS, OF COURSE!

BUT THE "RESTRUCTURING" WENT FARTHER AND FASTER THAN ANYONE EXPECTED...

1989 - MAJOR ELECTIONS ARE HELD IN THE U.S.S.R. AND OTHER EASTERN BLOC COUNTRIES. COMMUNIST CANDIDATES *LOSE* DECISIVELY. *LITHUANIA, LATVIA, ESTONIA,* AND *GEORGIA* DECLARE INDEPENDENCE FROM THE SOVIET UNION.

UH-OH... PERESTROIKA'S GETTING OUT OF HAND!

GORBACHEV DECIDES THAT THE U.S.S.R. MUST CONCENTRATE *EXCLUSIVELY* ON ITS *OWN PROBLEMS*. HE ANNOUNCES:

THE U.S.S.R. WILL NO LONGER INTERVENE IN THE AFFAIRS OF INDEPENDENT NATIONS IN THE EASTERN BLOC!

A FEW *OTHER THINGS* HAPPENED IN 1989...

1989

MAY HUNGARY DISMANTLES ITS COMMUNIST PARTY AND OPENS ITS BORDERS TO AUSTRIA; THOUSANDS OF EAST GERMANS FLOOD THE BORDER, TRYING TO EMIGRATE.

JUNE THE SOLIDARITY MOVEMENT RESURFACES IN POLAND AND WINS ELECTIONS. LECH WAŁĘSA, SOLIDARITY'S LEADER, BECOMES PRIME MINISTER.

OCTOBER THE BERLIN WALL COMES DOWN. EAST AND WEST GERMANY ARE REUNITED.

NOVEMBER BULGARIAN COMMUNIST LEADER TODOR ZHIVKOV IS REMOVED FROM POWER AS A RESULT OF POPULAR DEMONSTRATIONS.

NOVEMBER "VELVET REVOLUTION" IN CZECHOSLOVAKIA. MASS DEMONSTRATIONS BRING DOWN THE COMMUNIST GOVERNMENT.

DECEMBER ROMANIAN THUG/VAMPIRE/DICTATOR NICOLAE CEAUSESCU FALLS FROM POWER, TRIES TO FLEE, IS CAPTURED, TRIED, AND EXECUTED ON NATIONAL T.V. RATINGS SOAR.

OVER THE NEXT SEVERAL YEARS, COMMUNIST PARTIES WERE *OUTLAWED* IN SOME COUNTRIES, *RENAMED* IN OTHERS, *RESHAPED* IN STILL OTHERS.

IN AUGUST, 1991, OLD-LINE *SOVIET BOSSES* TRIED TO *OVERTHROW* GORBACHEV'S GOVERNMENT.

THE PEOPLE OF MOSCOW FACED DOWN THE TANKS, AND THE COUP FAILED.

HOWEVER, PEOPLE RESPONDED SO SEVERELY TO THIS REACTIONARY ATTEMPT TO HALT REFORM THAT THE COUP *DID* SUCCEED IN BRINGING ABOUT A *MAJOR CHANGE...*

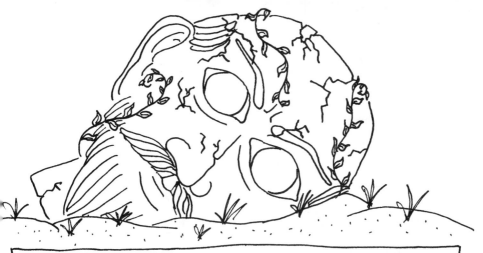

THE FALL OF THE COMMUNIST PARTY IN THE U.S.S.R.

SOVIET REPUBLICS BROKE AWAY AND DECLARED INDE-PENDENCE, AND SOON...

CRRACKK!

WE WERE IN A WHOLE NEW BALLGAME.

NEW BALLGAME? DID THE *OLD* GAME USE A BALL?

CHAPTER TEN

THE NEW GAME

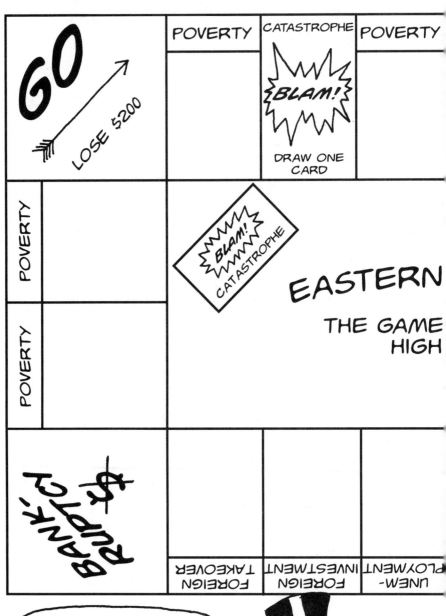

HYPER-NATIONALISM	OLD COMMIE BUREAUCRATS	NEW POLITICAL SYSTEM

INFLATION

STAY 5 TURNS OR UNTIL CURRENCY IS WORTHLESS

WAR

ETHNIC CONFLICT

EUROPE

OF POLITICAL STAKES

FOREIGN AID $

GIVE IT BACK

DRAW ONE CARD

$

FOREIGN AID

LABOR STRIKE

DEBT

STAY 5 TURNS OR UNTIL YOU PAY EVERYBODY BACK FOR EVERYTHING

SHOULDN'T THERE BE A *"FAT CITY"* SQUARE SOMEPLACE?

THE FALL OF THE SOVIET EMPIRE WAS MET WITH CELEBRATION!

SOON ENOUGH, HOWEVER, THE HAPPY PARTIERS WOKE UP AND LOOKED AROUND.

WHEN THEY LOOKED AROUND, WHAT THEY SAW WAS...

"WHAT WE THOUGHT WAS A HOUSE IN NEED OF REPAIR WAS ACTUALLY A RUIN."

- VACLAV HAVEL

POVERTY:

COUNTRIES SUCH AS ALBANIA, ROMANIA, AND BULGARIA, LACKING NATURAL RESOURCES OR RICH FARMLAND, WERE STILL POOR. INDEPENDENCE FROM THE SOVIET UNION ALSO MEANT AN END TO CHEAP RAW MATERIALS.

COLLECTIVE FARMING HAD IMPROVED PRODUCTION, BUT NOT ENOUGH.

YEW KIN KEEP SQUEEZIN' THAT TURNIP ALL YEW WANT...

MEANWHILE, MASSIVE INDUSTRIALIZATION HAD LEFT THESE COUNTRIES DEEPLY IN DEBT.

ER... I'M A LITTLE SHORT ON *DOLLARS*. WOULD YOU CONSIDER TAKING BULGARIAN *LEVAS* INSTEAD?

WHICH, IN TURN, MADE THE INTERNATIONAL VALUE OF THEIR NATIONAL CURRENCIES PLUMMET.

TATTERED CONSTITUTIONS:

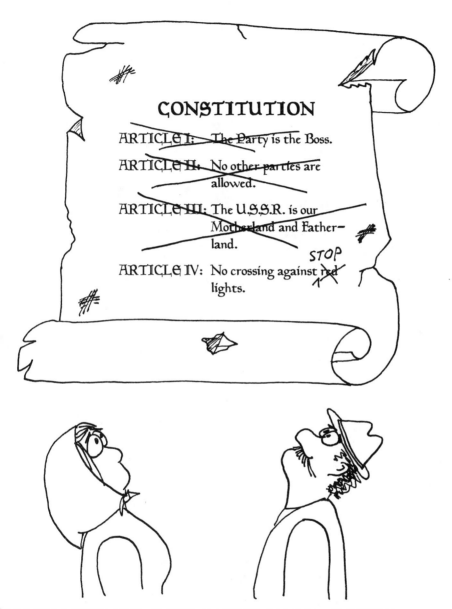

CONSTITUTION

ARTICLE I: ~~The Party is the Boss.~~

ARTICLE II: ~~No other parties are allowed.~~

ARTICLE III: ~~The U.S.S.R. is our Motherland and Fatherland.~~

ARTICLE IV: No crossing against ~~red~~ STOP lights.

WHICH LEFT BIG GAPS IN THE LEGAL SYSTEM.

IN SOME COUNTRIES, SUCH AS ALBANIA, THE LEGAL SYSTEM PRACTICALLY COLLAPSED. BY 1992 THERE WERE FOOD RIOTS, LOOTING, AND THEFT OF EMERGENCY SUPPLIES BY ORGANIZED GANGS, AND MOB RULE IN ALBANIAN CITIES.

PARLIAMENTS

WHICH USED TO HAVE NO REAL POWER BUT SUDDENLY HAD TO MAKE *REAL DECISIONS.*

THIS MEANT THAT THESE GOVERNING BODIES NEEDED TO LEARN THE NICETIES OF PARLIAMENTARY PROCEDURE.

MULTI-PARTY SYSTEMS

WHICH WERE A WELCOME RELIEF FROM ONE-PARTY DOMINANCE BY THE COMMUNIST PARTY, BUT WHICH SOMETIMES BECAME UNWIELDY...

INCLUDING SOME OLD FRIENDS WITH NEW FACES

NEW NAMES WITH OLD FACES

WHILE MANY OLD-LINE COMMUNIST LEADERS WERE DEPOSED OR ELECTED OUT OF OFFICE, SOME STAYED IN OFFICE OR WERE RE-ELECTED AFTER A SHORT TIME.

MEANWHILE, THE HUGE, NOT VERY EFFICIENT *BUREAU-CRACIES* THAT ADMINISTERED DAY-TO-DAY LIFE IN EASTERN EUROPE REMAINED LARGELY IN PLACE.

HI! I'M YOUR NEW *ASSISTANT CHIEF PERMIT OFFICER.*

AREN'T YOU THE *OLD* ASSISTANT CHIEF PERMIT OFFICER?

WELL, I'M THE SAME *PERSON* AS YOUR OLD ASSISTANT CHIEF PERMIT OFFICER- BUT *HE* WAS A COMMUNIST, WHEREAS *I* AM A *FREE MARKET CAPITALIST.*

OH.

MANY OF THESE BUREAUCRATS, KNOWN AS *NOMENCLATURA*, HAD BEEN IN POSITIONS TO PROFIT UNDER COMMUNISM - WHICH MEANT THAT THEY WERE AMONG THE FEW WHO COULD AFFORD TO BUY BUSINESSES AND PROPERTY UNDER PRIVATIZATION - AND SO PROFIT UNDER CAPITALISM, TOO.

AND BY THE WAY, I'VE ALSO OPENED UP A LITTLE *GROCERY STORE CHAIN.* I THINK YOU'LL LIKE IT - IT'S THE ONLY STORE IN TOWN.

133

FOR THE COMMON PERSON LIVING IN THESE COUNTRIES, THE RAPID, INCESSANT CHANGES IN GOVERNMENT, LAW, AND PROCEDURE BRED CONFUSION AND UNCERTAINTY.

135

ECONOMIC TRANSITION

UNDER THE COMMUNIST SYSTEM, AS WE HAVE SEEN, THE ECONOMY TENDED TO STAGNATE, AND MANY PEOPLE LIVED DIFFICULT LIVES.

WITH THE OVERTHROW OF COMMUNIST PARTIES EVERY-WHERE, THAT SYSTEM BECAME DISCREDITED, AND THE REGION WAS READY TO WELCOME A NEW IDEA...

UNDER THE COMMUNIST SYSTEM, EVERYONE WAS GUAR-ANTEED A PLACE TO LIVE, AND SO MOST LAWS FAVORED TENANTS.

UNDER *FREE MARKET CAPITALISM,* LAWS ARE CHANG-ING TO FAVOR *LANDLORDS.*

IN MOST COMMUNIST COUNTRIES, NO ONE WAS ABLE TO COLLECT MUCH WEALTH, EXCEPT FOR A FEW ELITE COMMUNIST PARTY MEMBERS.

UNDER FREE MARKET CAPITALISM, *ANYONE CAN GET RICH!* (THOUGH IN PRACTICE, WEALTH TENDS TO BECOME CONCENTRATED IN THE HANDS OF A FEW.)

SO, WITH THE INTRODUCTION OF WESTERN-STYLE FREE MARKET ECONOMY, MANY PEOPLE IN EASTERN EUROPE WERE ALSO INTRODUCED TO SEVERAL OTHER WESTERN CONCEPTS:

UNEMPLOYMENT

CLOSED
DUE TO LOW PROFITS

HOMELESSNESS

SOUP KITCHEN

DESTITUTION

MEANWHILE, MANY INDUSTRIES ARE TOO INEFFICIENT OR OUTDATED TO BE PROFITABLE. THOSE INDUSTRIES THAT COULD BE PROFITABLE ARE BEING BOUGHT BY FOREIGN FIRMS.

HEY, WHAT ARE ALL THESE **GERMANS** DOING HERE?

DIDN'T WE KICK THEM OUT IN '45?

BUT THEY **NEED** FOREIGN INVESTMENT, TO REBUILD FACTORIES, CREATE JOBS, AND CREATE A TAX BASE FOR **NEW, STRUGGLING GOVERNMENTS!**

HE'S RIGHT...

AND IF WE MAKE A LITTLE *PROFIT* OFF IT BACK AT THE *HOME OFFICE* IN ST. LOUIS, WELL, IS THAT SO WRONG?

BUT WHAT ABOUT ALL THE MONEY THAT'S BEING TAKEN *OUT* OF OUR COUNTRIES?

AND SOCIAL PROGRAMS THAT ARE CUT!

AND EVERYTHING'S MORE EXPENSIVE!

AND OUR ENVIRONMENTS ARE STILL BEING POLLUTED!

AND MORE AND MORE OF US WORK FOR...

AND WHILE ALL THE COUNTRIES DEAL WITH DIFFICULT ECONOMIC QUESTIONS, SOME MUST DEAL WITH...

BORDER DISPUTES

WITH INDEPENDENCE COMES NATIONALISM.

AND WITH NATIONALISM, SOMETIMES, COMES *HYPERNATIONALISM.*

AND HYPERNATIONALISTS WON'T REST UNTIL POLITICAL BORDERS MATCH ETHNIC BORDERS. SO:

1. THERE IS A LARGE ALBANIAN POPULATION IN THE YUGOSLAV/SERBIAN PROVINCE OF KOSOVO. BOTH SERBS AND ALBANIANS CLAIM THE TERRITORY.

2. MANY HUNGARIANS LIVE IN SLOVAKIA, AND MANY SLOVAKS LIVE IN HUNGARY, LEAVING THE REGION OF THE CARPATHIAN MOUNTAINS IN DISPUTE.

3. BOTH HUNGARIANS AND ROMANIANS LIVE IN THE ROMANIAN DISTRICT OF TRANSYLVANIA; BOTH COUNTRIES ARE PUTTING CLAIMS TO THE REGION.

4. THERE IS A REGION IN *GREECE* CALLED "MACEDONIA", AS WELL AS A STATE IN THE *FORMER YUGOSLAVIA* CALLED "MACEDONIA". AS A RESULT, THE INDEPENDENT STATE MUST BE INTERNATIONALLY RECOGNIZED WITH THE FORMAL TITLE OF *THE FORMER YUGO-SLAV REPUBLIC OF MACEDONIA*.

5. THERE ARE ALSO RELIGIOUS TROUBLES: ORTHODOX CHRISTIANS AND MUSLIMS ARE AT ODDS IN BULGARIA.

AND NOT ONLY BORDER DISPUTES, BUT SOMETIMES...

SECESSION

BOTH PEACEFUL...

THE URBAN, INDUSTRIAL <u>CZECHS</u> AND THE RURAL, AGRI-
CULTURAL <u>SLOVAKS</u> HAVE A LONG HISTORY OF PEACEFUL
COEXISTENCE.

THEY UNITED DURING WORLD WAR ONE TO FORM ONE
NATION, HOPING TO RESIST FURTHER SUBJUGATION BY
EMPIRES.

DURING THE COMMUNIST YEARS, HOWEVER, THE
CZECHS AND SLOVAKS BEGAN TO GROW IMPATIENT WITH
EACH OTHER.

THEY MAKE LAWS FOR CITY FOLK!

THEY KEEP ASKING FOR MORE MONEY!

AFTER INDEPENDENCE, CZECHS AND SLOVAKS FOUND
THEMSELVES BLOCKING EACH OTHER'S POLITICAL GES-
TURES, RESULTING IN PARLIAMENTARY DEADLOCK.

IN THE SUMMER OF 1992, THE TWO REGIONS VOTED
TO SPLIT APART INTO TWO NATIONS: THE CZECH REPUB-
LIC AND SLOVAKIA. NOT A SHOT WAS FIRED.

AND SECESSION, NOT SO PEACEFUL

ARE WE TALKING ABOUT YUGOSLAVIA?

AFRAID SO.

WITH INDEPENDENCE FEVER AND NATIONALISM SWEEP-ING EASTERN EUROPE, THE PEOPLES OF SEVERAL REGIONS DECIDED TO ATTEMPT NATIONHOOD.

IN THE SUMMER OF 1991, THE AUTONOMOUS REGIONS OF CROATIA AND SLOVENIA VOTED TO SECEDE FROM YUGOSLAVIA.

CROATIA FOR THE CROATS

SLOVENIA FOR THE SLOVENES

THE MOVEMENTS FOR SECESSION HAD BEEN INCREAS-ING EVER SINCE TITO'S DEATH IN 1980. HOWEVER, AN-OTHER GROUP ALSO HAD NATIONALIST ASPIRATIONS...

IN YUGOSLAVIA, SERBS MADE UP 40% OF THE POPULATION AND *DOMINATED* THE GOVERNMENT.

AND WE *LIKE* IT THAT WAY!

WITH THE BREAKUP OF THE U.S.S.R., THE DREAM OF A *GREATER SERBIA* (TRANSLATION: ALL OF YUGOSLAVIA UNDER SERB RULE) FINALLY SEEMED WITHIN REACH.

THE SERBS DIDN'T TAKE SECESSION KINDLY.

YOU DIDN'T LET A BUNCHA DAMN *CONFEDERATES* BREAK APART *YOUR* COUNTRY, DID YOU?

GREATER SERBIA FOR THE SERBS

FURTHERMORE...

THERE ARE *SERBS* LIVING IN *CROATIA!* THEY'LL BE *OPPRESSED*, JUST AS THEY WERE IN *WORLD WAR TWO!*

SERBS FEARED ANOTHER OUTBREAK OF FASCIST-STYLE HYPERNATIONALISM BY CROATS. SO...

THE *YPA* (YUGOSLAV PEOPLE'S ARMY) ENTERED SLOVENIA AND CROATIA WITH THE NOBLE MISSION OF *KEEPING YUGOSLAVIA TOGETHER*.

RIGHT AWAY, CROATS AND SLOVENES DESERTED THE YPA IN LARGE NUMBERS, LEAVING IT DOMINATED ALL THE MORE BY SERBS.

SO, SOON ENOUGH, THE *YUGOSLAV PEOPLE'S ARMY* BECAME, IN EFFECT, THE *ARMY OF GREATER SERBIA*.

THE WAR IN SLOVENIA LASTED 10 DAYS...

WHO'DA THUNK THESE SLOVENES WOULD BE SO *STUBBORN*?

...AND ENDED IN SERBIAN DEFEAT.

THE WAR IN CROATIA LASTED UNTIL 1992, WHEN INTERNATIONAL DIPLOMATS FROM THE EUROPEAN COMMUNITY HELPED NEGOTIATE AN UNEASY CEASEFIRE.

TRUCE?

YEAH. SURE. WHATEVER.

BUT THEN, IN APRIL 1992, ONE OTHER AUTONOMOUS REGION OF YUGOSLAVIA CAUGHT THE INDEPENDENCE ITCH:

BOSNIA FOR THE BOSNIANS

MUSLIMS!

SINCE THE FALL OF WORLD COMMUNISM HAS DE-PRIVED WESTERN COUNTRIES OF THEIR CONVENIENT SCAPEGOAT/DEMON/ENEMY, MANY PEOPLE IN THE U.S. AND EUROPE HAVE REDIRECTED THEIR UNREASONED PREJUDICE TOWARD MUSLIMS, ACCEPTING THE STE-REOTYPICAL FICTION THAT ALL MUSLIMS ARE RELI-GIOUS EXTREMISTS AND PROTO-TERRORISTS. THE SERBS HAVE NEATLY EXPLOITED THIS.

THEY PROBABLY WANT A *FANATIC THEOCRACY* LIKE *IRAN!*

ISLAMIC STATE? I'M NOT EVEN *RELIGIOUS!*

BY 1990, BOSNIA WAS POPULATED BY:

- ABOUT 45% MUSLIMS — (THAT IS, PEOPLE WHOSE *ANCESTORS* CONVERTED TO ISLAM)

- ABOUT 30% SERBS — (THAT IS, PEOPLE WHOSE *ANCESTORS* REMAINED ORTHODOX CHRISTIAN)

- ABOUT 17% CROATS — (THAT IS, PEOPLE WHOSE *ANCESTORS* REMAINED ROMAN CATHOLIC)

- AND ABOUT 8% GYPSIES, JEWS, ALBANIANS, ETC.

WERE THEY ALL DEVOTED FOLLOWERS OF THOSE FAITHS?

- NO. SOME WERE RELIGIOUS; MANY WEREN'T.

DID THEY LIVE SEPARATELY?

- NO. ALL WERE MIXED TOGETHER AND SCATTERED ALL OVER BOSNIA.

DID THEY SPEAK DIFFERENT LANGUAGES OR USE DIFFERENT ALPHABETS?

- NO. ALL SPOKE SERBO-CROATIAN. BOTH CYRILLIC AND RO-MAN ALPHABETS WERE USED IN BOSNIA, WITH WESTERN BOSNIAN SERBS USING THE ROMAN ALPHABET (AS CROATIA DOES), AND EASTERN BOSNIAN CROATS USING THE CYRILLIC (AS SERBIA DOES). SLANG FROM CROATIAN AND SERBIAN FREELY MIXED WITH LOCAL BOSNIAN DIA-LECTS, AS WITH THE WORD "FRIEND":

HIYA, *PRITEL!*

HOWDY, *DROOG!*

(CROATIAN)

(SERBIAN)

155

HOWEVER:

ALL DURING THE 1980'S - AFTER TITO'S DEATH - *SERBIAN* SERBS HAD BEEN FOMENTING ETHNIC AWARENESS IN *BOSNIAN* SERBS.

VITH SERBIAN ETHNIC NATIONALISM ON THE RISE...

BOSNIAN CROATS AND MUSLIMS BEGAN POLARIZING NTO NATIONALIST PARTIES OF THEIR OWN.

N 1990, A REFORM PARTY, RUNNING ON AN ANTI-NATION-ALIST PLATFORM, WAS SOUNDLY DEFEATED BY THE THREE ETHNIC PARTIES.

157

WAIT A MINUTE! I'M ONE OF THE BOSNIAKS YOU'RE CALLING "MUSLIM", AND *I DON'T WANT* BOSNIA TO BE SOME ISLAMIC OR MUSLIM-ONLY STATE!

WHAT *DO* YOU WANT?

I WANT BOSNIA (AND ITS CAPITAL, SARAJEVO) TO CONTINUE BEING MULTI-ETHNIC AND MULTI-RELIGIOUS, WITH SERBS, CROATS, MUSLIMS, JEWS, GYPSIES, AND ALL THE OTHER KINDS OF BOSNIANS LIVING THERE, JUST AS THEY DID FOR HUNDREDS OF YEARS!

THAT'S WHAT I WANT, TOO. SO EVEN THOUGH THEY'RE TELLING ME THAT I'M A BOSNIAN *SERB*, I'VE JOINED THE MUSLIMS.

ME TOO! EVEN THOUGH THEY CALL ME A BOSNIAN *CROAT*.

THE BIG SECRET:

WHILE INTERNATIONAL MEDIA KEEP REFERRING TO THE "BOSNIAN MUSLIM GOVERNMENT" OR THE "MUSLIM-DOMINATED ARMY", BOTH GOVERNMENT AND ARMY ARE MADE UP OF *BOSNIAKS* - MUSLIM, SERB, AND CROAT - WHO FAVOR THE CREATION OF BOSNIA AS A *MULTI-ETHNIC STATE.*

MULTI-ETHNIC STATE? YOU MEAN WHERE POLITICAL BOUNDARIES DON'T *HAVE* TO MATCH ETHNIC BOUNDARIES?

YUP. YOU MIGHT CALL IT *ANTI-HYPERNATIONALISM.*

158

NONETHELESS, THE PREDOMINANTLY LOWER AND LOWER-MIDDLE-CLASS BOSNIAN SERBS WERE EASILY STIRRED UP AGAINST THE PREDOMINANTLY UPPER AND UPPER-MIDDLE-CLASS MUSLIMS.

MULTI-ETHNIC STATE?! HOGWASH! MUSLIM RICH PEOPLE HAVE ALWAYS OPPRESSED POOR SERBS! SEEN ONE MUSLIM, SEEN 'EM ALL! *GREATER SERBIA* FOREVER!

SO, IN APRIL 1992, WHEN THE GOVERNMENT OF BOSNIA-HERZEGOVINA DECLARED INDEPENDENCE (RATHER THAN REMAIN IN A "RUMP" YUGOSLAVIA DOMINATED BY SERBS), MANY BOSNIANS SAID:

RIGHT ON!

MANY SAID:

HUH?

AND MANY BOSNIAN *SERBS* SAID:

NO WAY!

SOME BOSNIAN SERBS FORMED PARAMILITARY GROUPS...

...WHICH THE SERBIAN ARMY (OOPS - WE MEAN THE YUGOSLAV PEOPLE'S ARMY) QUICKLY BEGAN TO ARM AND TRAIN.

ATTACKING BOSNIA? WE'RE NOT ATTACKING BOSNIA. WE'RE SIMPLY SUPPORTING THE EF-FORTS OF *PATRIOTIC FREEDOM FIGHT-ERS*. AND ANYWAY, OUR ARMY WAS STILL ON ITS WAY HOME FROM FIGHTING *CROATIA*, SO WE WERE IN THE NEIGHBORHOOD...

SOON ENOUGH, HOWEVER, THE LARGE, WELL-ARMED SERBIAN YUGOSLAV ARMY BEGAN BATTLING THE SMALL, POORLY-ARMED BOSNIAN FORCES. (IN FACT, THE BOSNIAN ARMY CONSISTED MOSTLY OF THE BOSNIAN <u>POLICE FORCE</u>.)

160

DID THE WORLD JUST STAND BY AND LET THIS HAPPEN?

WELL, WITH TYPICAL FOREIGN-POLICY INSIGHT, THE U.S. AND THE U.N. IMPOSED AN EMBARGO ON WEAPONS SALES TO ALL COMBATING FACTIONS - WHICH MADE SURE THAT THE UNEQUAL BATTLE *STAYED* UNEQUAL.

AND THE U.N. DID SEND IN A FEW PEACEKEEPING TROOPS.

KABOOM!

BLAM!?

POW!

C'MON YOU GUYS, CUT IT OUT!

I MEAN IT!

JUST KNOCK IT OFF!

PZZINNG!

UN

WHY WERE U.S. ACTIONS SO TIMID AND INCONCLUSIVE?

WELL, THE U.S. DOESN'T MUCH LIKE TO INTERVENE IN THE INTERNAL AFFAIRS OF OTHER COUNTRIES.
(*UNLESS,* OF COURSE, THOSE COUNTRIES HAVE IMPORTANT NATURAL RESOURCES, LIKE KUWAIT, OR STRATEGIC IMPORTANCE, LIKE NICARAGUA OR VIETNAM.)

RE-ELECT ME

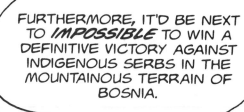

FURTHERMORE, IT'D BE NEXT TO *IMPOSSIBLE* TO WIN A DEFINITIVE VICTORY AGAINST INDIGENOUS SERBS IN THE MOUNTAINOUS TERRAIN OF BOSNIA.

AND ANYWAY, THEY'RE JUST MUSLIMS.

THE SERBS WOULD PROBABLY HAVE OVERRUN AND CONQUERED BOSNIA, BUT THE BOSNIANS FOUND AN ALLY IN THE FORMER ENEMIES OF SERBIA:

THE CROATS FOUGHT THE SERBS ALONGSIDE THE BOSNIANS FOR A WHILE, UNTIL THE CROATS GOT A NEW IDEA:

SO THE CROATS, WHILE STILL FIGHTING OFF THE SERBS, ALSO TOOK LARGE PARTS OF BOSNIA AND DECLARED THEM PART OF CROATIA.

BY 1994, BOSNIA LOOKED LIKE THIS:

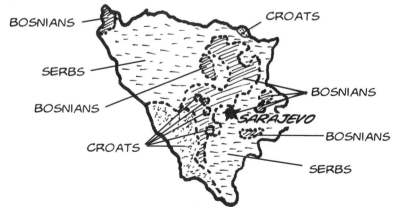

AND THE CRIES OF "CROATIA FOR CROATS" AND "SERBIA FOR SERBIANS" HAD GIVEN RISE TO A NEW WAVE OF...

163

"ETHNIC CLEANSING"

IN MOST WARS OF TERRITORIAL AMBITION, THE OBJECT IS TO CONQUER AND SUBJUGATE PEOPLES.

IN BOSNIA, HOWEVER, THE SERBS — FOLLOWING THE SHINING EXAMPLES OF NAZI GERMANY, TURKEY, ISRAEL, THE UNITED STATES, AND OTHERS — CHOSE TO SUPPORT THEIR TERRITORIAL CLAIMS BY RIDDING THE COUNTRYSIDE OF ANYONE WHO WASN'T A SERB.

ETHNIC CLEANSING — ALSO KNOWN AS "ETHNIC EXCLUSIVISM" AND "PURSUING A HOMOGENEOUS STATE" — REQUIRES NOT JUST BATTLE, BUT ALSO TERRORISM, SYSTEMATIC RAPE, MUTILATION, PRISON CAMPS, AND THE DELIBERATE DESTRUCTION OF HOMES AND DRIVING AWAY OF CIVILIANS.

THE PROGRAM ALSO HAD THE <u>DOUBLE</u> <u>ADVANTAGES</u> OF DESTROYING THE BOSNIAN ECONOMY AND DE-STROYING THE MULTI-ETHNIC POPULATION BASE, THUS UNDERMINING BOSNIA'S CLAIMS FOR INDEPENDENCE AS A MULTI-ETHNIC STATE.

THE CROATS SOON FOLLOWED SUIT.

AND, FINALLY, THE SERBS GOT WHAT THEY WANTED: SOME BOSNIAN MUSLIM EXTREMISTS BEGAN PRACTIC-ING ETHNIC CLEANSING AGAINST SERBS.

SEE? WE **TOLD** YOU THEY WERE FANATICS!

THE RESULTS:

- 200,000 DEAD

- 50,000 WOMEN RAPED

- FAMILY AGAINST FAMILY, NEIGHBOR AGAINST NEIGHBOR

- RAMPANT RACISM

- DESTRUCTION OF A MULTI-ETHNIC STATE

- ONCE-PROSPEROUS YUGOSLAV ECONOMY REDUCED BY 85% — NOW AS POOR AS ALBANIA

- HOMELESS, DESTITUTE REFUGEES NUMBER IN THE HUNDREDS OF THOUSANDS

BUT...

ISN'T THERE *PEACE* NOW?

TECHNICALLY, YES.

IN NOVEMBER 1995, THE UNITED STATES AND NATO FINALLY DECIDED TO DO WHAT VICTORIOUS EMPIRES HAVE ALWAYS DONE: *REARRANGE BORDERS.*

WHAT A CONCEPT!

JUST LOOK WHAT THEY DID TO THE WEST BANK!

DON'T GET HIM STARTED!

PREZ BILL

SO THEY FORCED THE GOVERNMENTS OF SERBIA, CROATIA, AND BOSNIA TO NEGOTIATE AN AGREEMENT SPLITTING BOSNIA-HERZEGOVINA INTO SEPARATE REGIONS: A *BOSNIAN SERB STATE* AND A *CROAT-MUSLIM FEDERATION.*

BOSNIAN SERB STATE

MUSLIM-CROAT FEDERATION

BIHAĆ · BANJA LUCA · SARAJEVO ★ · GORAŽDE · MOSTAR

BOSNIA-HERZEGOVINA

SO EVERYONE GOT WHAT THEY WANTED, RIGHT?

WELL...

DID THE SERBS GET GREATER SERBIA?

NO.

DID THE BOSNIANS GET A UNIFIED, MULTI-ETHNIC BOSNIA?

NO.

DO ALL THE PEOPLE WHO WERE DRIVEN FROM THEIR HOMES GET TO GO HOME?

NO.

IN FACT, THE CREATION OF TWO ETHNOCENTRIC STATES HAS CREATED MANY THOUSAND *MORE* REFUGEES.

DO WAR CRIMINALS GET BROUGHT TO TRIAL?

- NO.

DOES THE TREATY RESOLVE ANY OF THE ISSUES THAT CAUSED THE TROUBLE IN THE FIRST PLACE?

- UH...NO...

SO DID *ANYBODY* GET WHAT THEY WANTED?

- OF COURSE: THE *UNITED STATES.*
POLITICIANS GOT TO *LOOK GOOD*...

I ♡ ☮

☆ CALL ME STATESMAN ☆

ME IN '96

NOBEL PRIZE, HERE WE COME!

...BECAUSE THEY SOLVED EVERYTHING WITHOUT COMMITTING THE U.S. MILITARY - EXCEPT OF COURSE THE 20,000 TROOPS WHO WILL STAFF THE "BUFFER ZONES" TO MAINTAIN THE PEACE - FOR AN *INDEFINITE PERIOD OF TIME.*

OKAY YOU GUYS. EASY, NOW. EASY...

AND, MORE IMPORTANTLY, THE AMERICAN PUBLIC (EX-CEPT, PERHAPS, FOR THE FAMILIES OF THOSE 20,000 TROOPS) GOT TO **REST EASY** KNOWING THAT THERE WAS NO MORE TROUBLE IN BOSNIA!

THE FUTURE

IN TIMES OF DISTRESS THE RISE OF HYPERNATIONALISM
AND THE FEAR OF ECONOMIC COLONIZATION GIVE RISE
TO A FAMLIAR POLICY:

PREJUDICE AGAINST GYPSIES AND OTHER ETHNIC GROUPS
IS WIDESPREAD THROUGHOUT HUNGARY, ROMANIA, AND
THE CZECH REPUBLIC.

WILL THERE BE MORE ETHNIC CLEANSING IN OTHER
COUNTRIES?

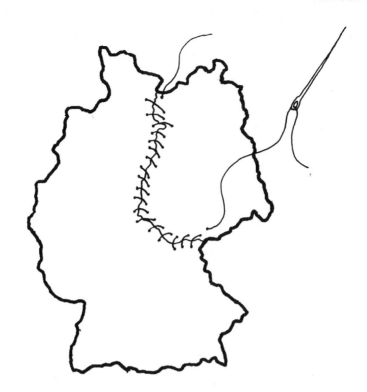

THE REUNIFICATION OF GERMANY HAS SENT SHIVERS DOWN THE SPINES OF MANY EUROPEANS WHO LOST FATHERS IN WORLD WAR TWO AND GRANDFATHERS IN WORLD WAR ONE.

GERMANY IS NOT HAVING AN EASY FINANCIAL TIME, AND IT'S HARD TO IMAGINE THE WORLD ALLOWING THE GROWTH OF A *FOURTH REICH* — BUT NOTHING IS IMPOSSIBLE.

ARE THE FREE-MARKET COUNTRIES TRYING TO *HELP*, OR SIMPLY TO *EXPLOIT* EASTERN EUROPE AND DEVELOP NEW MARKETS - OR NEW ECONOMIC COLONIES?

BOTH, PROBABLY. AND THE PEOPLE OF EASTERN EUROPE HAVE LITTLE CHOICE BUT TO ACCEPT IT EITHER WAY.

WILL NATIONALISTS, HYPERNATIONALISTS, AND EMPIRES KEEP REDRAWING THE BORDERS OF BOSNIA UNTIL THERE'S NO BOSNIA LEFT?

GREATER SERBIA FOREVER!

IS EASTERN EUROPE DESTINED ALWAYS TO BE NOTHING MORE THAN THE CROSSROADS, INTERSECTION, AND BATTLEGROUND OF EMPIRES?

SOUNDS GOOD.

OR IS THERE A PLACE IN THE FUTURE FOR:

A REGION OF MULTI-ETHNIC,
MULTINATIONAL, INDEPENDENT STATES,
ALL EXPERIMENTING WITH
NEW COMBINATIONS OF
SOCIAL, ECONOMIC, AND
GOVERNMENTAL FORMS,
CREATING NEW SYNTHE-
SES OF SOCIALISM AND
CAPITALISM,
LIVING IN PEACE
AMONGST THEM-
SELVES AND WITH
THE REST OF
THE WORLD

?

THE
END

SOME BOOKS

ANDERSON, M.S., *THE ASCENDANCY OF EUROPE 1815-1914*, LONDON: LONGMA 1985.

BLACK, CYRIL E., JONATHAN E. HELMREICH, ET AL., *REBIRTH: A HISTORY OF EUROPE SINCE WWII*, OXFORD: WESTRIEN PRESS, 1992.

BRADLEY, JOHN, *EASTERN EUROPE: THE ROAD TO DEMOCRACY*, NEW YORK. GLOUCESTER PRESS, 1990.

DONIA, ROBERT J. AND JOHN V.A. FINE, JR., *BOSNIA AND HERCEGOVINA: A TRADITION BETRAYED*, NEW YORK, COLUMBIA UNIVERSITY PRESS, 1994.

ECHIKSON, WILLIAM, *LIGHTING THE NIGHT: REVOLUTION IN EASTERN EU- ROPE*, NEW YORK: WILLIAM MORROW & CO., 1990.

GILBERT, FELIX, *THE END OF THE EUROPEAN ERA*, NEW YORK: WW NORTON, 19

GOLDBERG, GEORGE, *THE PEACE TO END PEACE*, NEW YORK: HARCOURT, BRACE & WORLD INC., 1969.

HELMREICH, PAUL, *FROM PARIS TO SEVRES*, COLUMBUS: OHIO STATE UNIVER- SITY PRESS, 1974.

KINDER, HERMANN AND WERNER HILGEMANN, *THE ANCHOR ATLAS OF WORLD HISTORY*, (V. I AND II), NEW YORK: ANCHOR PRESS, 1978.

LEWIS, PAUL G., *CENTRAL EUROPE SINCE 1945*, LONDON: LONGMANS, 1994.

MAGOCSI, PAUL ROBERT, *HISTORICAL ATLAS OF EAST CENTRAL EUROPE*, SEATTLE: UNIVERSITY OF WASHINGTON PRESS, 1994.

MOJZES, PAUL, *YUGOSLAVIAN INFERNO*, NEW YORK: CONTINUUM, 1994.

NICOLSON, HAROLD, *PEACEMAKING 1919*, BOSTON: HOUGHTON MIFFLIN, 1933.

NOWAK, KARL FRIEDRICH, *VERSAILLES*, NEW YORK: PAYSON & CLARK, LTD., 1929.

NYROP, RICHARD (ED.), *CZECHOSLOVAKIA: A COUNTRY STUDY*, WASHINGTON D AMERICAN UNIVERSITY PRESS, 1981.

O'KEEFE, EUGENE ET AL., *AREA HANDBOOK FOR POLAND*, WASHINGTON DC: GOVERNMENT PUBLICATION OFFICE, 1973.

IBID., *AREA HANDBOOK FOR AUSTRIA*, WASHINGTON DC: US GOVERNMENT PU LICATION OFFICE, 1976.

IBID., *AREA HANDBOOK FOR HUNGARY*, WASHINGTON DC: US GOVERNMENT PUBLICATION OFFICE, 1973.

POUNDS, N.J.G., *AN HISTORICAL GEOGRAPHY OF EUROPE*, CAMBRIDGE: CU PRESS, 1990.

PRAGNICK, ALEX. N., *SERBS AND CROATS: THE STRUGGLE IN YUGOSLAVIA*, NEW YORK: HARCOURT, BRACE & JANOVICH, 1992.

SCHMITT, BERNADOTTE E. AND HAROLD C. VEDELER, *THE WORLD IN THE CRU CIBLE 1914-19*, NEW YORK: HARPER & ROW, 1984.

SHOEMAKER, M. WESLEY, PHD., *RUSSIA, EURASIAN STATES, AND EASTERN EUROPE 1994*, HARPERS FERRY: STRYKER-POST PUBLICATIONS, 1994.

SIMONS, THOMAS W. JR., *EASTERN EUROPE IN THE POSTWAR WORLD*, NEW YORK: ST. MARTIN'S PRESS, 1991.

STAVRIANOS, L.S., *THE BALKANS SINCE 1453*, NEW YORK: HOLT, RINEHART & WIN STON, 1958.

STEINBERG, S.H., *HISTORICAL TABLES 58 BC - AD 1961*, NEW YORK: ST. MARTIN'S PRESS, 1961.

SUGAR, PETER F. AND IVO JOHN LEDERER (EDS.), *NATIONALISM IN EASTERN EUROPE*, SEATTLE: UNIVERSITY OF WASHINGTON PRESS, 1981.

TOYNBEE, ARNOLD, *A STUDY OF HISTORY* (V. VIII), LONDON: OXFORD UNIVERSIT PRESS, 1954.

WALWORTH, ARUTH, *WILSON AND HIS PEACEMAKERS*, NEW YORK: WW NORTC 1986.

WEST, REBECCA, *BLACK LAMB AND GREY FALCON*, NEW YORK: PENGUIN, 1969

WESTOBY, ADAM, *COMMUNISM SINCE WWII*, NEW YORK: ST. MARTIN'S PRESS, 19

WETTERAU, BRUCE, *WORLD HISTORY: A DICTIONARY OF IMPORTANT PEOPLE, PLACES AND EVENTS FROM ANCIENT TIMES TO THE PRESENT*, NEW YORK: HENRY HOLD & CO., 1994.

YENNE, BILL (ED.), *FLAGS OF THE WORLD*, SECAUCUS NJ: CHARTWELL BOOKS, 1993.

INDEX

WHAT'S NEW?

THE BLACK HOLOCAUST FOR BEGINNERS

By S.E. Anderson; Illustrated by the Cro-maat Collective and Vanessa Holley

The Black Holocaust, a travesty that killed no less than 50 million African human beings, is the most underreported major event in world history. But it won't be for long. *The Black Holocaust For Beginners* — part indisputably documented chronicle, part passionately engaging narrative, will put this tragic event in plain sight where it belongs!
Trade paper, $11.00 ($15.75 Can., £6.99 UK), ISBN 0-86316-178-2

JAZZ FOR BEGINNERS

By Ron David; Illustrated by Vanessa Holley

An amazingly thorough guide to Jazz that is as full of blood, guts and humor as the music it describes.
Trade paper, $11.00 ($15.75 Can., £6.99 UK), ISBN 0-86316-165-0

BLACK PANTHERS FOR BEGINNERS

By Herb Boyd; Illustrated by Lance Tooks

The late 1960s, when the Panthers captured the imagination of the nation's youth, was a time of revolution. While their furious passage was marked by death, destruction, and government sabotage, the Panthers left an instructive legacy for anyone who dares to challenge the system. But don't settle for half-truths or fictionalized accounts. Learn the whole story, the way it really happened, by American Book Award winner Herb Boyd.
Trade paper, $11.00 ($15.75 Can., £6.99 UK), ISBN 0-86316-196-0

DOMESTIC VIOLENCE FOR BEGINNERS

By Alisa Del Tufo; Illustrated by Barbara Henry

Why do men hurt women — and why has so little been done about it? What can be done? A no-holds barred look at the causes and effects of spousal abuse — an epidemic by any standards that is still ignored. This book is not a luxury; it should be part of a survival kit given to everyone who buys a Marriage License. Your life — or your child's life — could depend on it.
Trade paper, $11.00 ($15.75 Can., £6.99 UK), ISBN 0-86316-1173-1

WRITERS AND READERS PUBLISHING, INC.
625 Broadway, New York, NY 10012

**To order, or for a free catalog, please call (212) 982-3158;
fax (212) 777-4924. MC/Visa accepted.**

183

SUBSTITUTE!

And knowledge, as you will discover in our "Documentary Comic Books," is fun! Each book is painstakingly researched, humorously written and illustrated in whatever style best suits the subject at hand.

MAKING
COMPLEX SUBJECTS
SIMPLE
AND
SERIOUS SUBJECTS
FUN!!!

That's **Writers and Readers,** where **For Beginners**™ books began! Remember, if it doesn't say...

... it's not an <u>original</u> **For Beginners** ™ book!

Chomsky For Beginners

by David Cogswell; illustrated by Paul Gordon

Race For Beginners

by S.E. Anderson Illustrated by The Cro-Maat Collective

McLuhan For Beginners

by W. Terrence Gordon; illustrated by Susan Willmarth

I-Ching For Beginners

by Brandon Toropov; illustrated by John Kane

The History of Eastern Europe For Beginners

by Beck, Mast and Tapper

HOW TO GET GREAT THINKERS TO COME TO YOUR HOME...

To order any current titles of Writers and Readers **For Beginners**™ books, please fill out the coupon below and enclose a check made out to **Writers and Readers Publishing, Inc.** To order by phone (with Master Card or Visa), or to receive a <u>free catalog</u> of all our **For Beginners**™ books, please call (212) 982-3158.

Price per book: $11.00

Individual Order Form   (clip out or copy complete page)

Book Title	Quantity	Amount
	Sub Total:	
N.Y. residents add 8 1/4% sales tax		
Shipping & Handling ($3.00 for the first book; $.60 for each additional book)		
	TOTAL	

Name _____

Address _____

City _____ **State** _____ **Zip Code** _____

Phone number (___) _____

MC / VISA (circle one)   Account # _____ **Expires** _____

Addiction & Recovery ($11.00)
African History ($9.95)
Arabs & Israel ($12.00)
Architecture ($11.00)
Babies ($9.95)
Biology ($11.00)
Black History ($9.95)
Black Holocaust ($11.00)
Black Panthers ($11.00)
Black Women ($9.95)
Brecht ($9.95)
Buddha ($11.00)
Chomsky ($11.00)
Classical Music ($9.95)
Computers ($11.00)
Derrida ($11.00)
DNA ($9.95)
Domestic Violence ($11.00)
Elvis ($6.95)
Erotica ($7.95)
Food ($7.95)
Foucault ($9.95)
Freud ($9.95)
Health Care ($9.95)
Heidegger ($9.95)
Hemingway ($9.95)
History of Clowns ($11.00)
I-Ching ($11.00)
Ireland ($9.95)
Islam ($9.95)
Jazz ($11.00)
Jewish Holocaust ($11.00)
J.F.K. ($9.95)
Judaism ($11.00)
Jung ($11.00)
Kierkegaard ($11.00)
Lacan ($11.00)
Malcolm X ($9.95)
Mao ($9.95)
Martial Arts ($11.00)
Miles Davis ($9.00)
Nietzsche ($11.00)
Opera ($11.00)
Orwell ($4.95)
Pan-Africanism ($9.95)
Philosophy ($11.00)
Plato ($11.00)
Psychiatry ($9.95)
Rainforests ($7.95)
Sartre ($11.00)
Saussure ($11.00)
Sex ($9.95)
Shakespeare ($11.00)
Structuralism ($11.00)
UNICEF ($11.00)
United Nations ($11.00)
World War II ($8.95)
Zen ($11.00)

Send check or money order to: **Writers and Readers Publishing**, P.O. Box 461 Village Station, New York, NY 10014 (212) 982-3158, fx (212) 777-4924; In the U.K: **Airlift Book Company**, 8, The Arena, Mollison Ave., Enfield, EN3 7NJ, England 0181.804.0044. Or contact us for a <u>FREE</u> <u>CATALOG</u> of all our *For Beginners*™ titles.